Motorcycles, Planes, & Revolution

To Christene Symnes

Michael J. Hanley

by Michael J. Hanley

Published by:

    Autumn Woods Studio
    Elkhorn, Wisconsin 53121 USA

    For information about special discounts for bulk purchases, please contact the
    author at mikeh@motorcyclesplanesandrevolution.com

ISBN   978-0-9831737-1-7

Library of Congress Control Number: 2010917616

Cover: "Following the Footsteps of Freedom" original art concept by Michael J Hanley,
Photoshop work by Mary Brandes.
At left: Spirit of '76 by A. M. Willard done in 1876, from the US Government Archives.
At right: Author and daughter riding Harley-Davidson as seen on page 2 of this book.
Background: An Accurate Map of the Country round Boston in New England by Archibald
Hamilton in 1776, engraved for the Town & Country Magazine in London 1776, courtesy
American Geographical Society Library, University of Wisconsin-Milwaukee Libraries, as
seen on page 20 of this book.

I would like to dedicate this book to my loving wife Dee, who has stood by her man through good times and bad these last forty years. She has encouraged my woodworking and allowed me the freedom to ride, and I could not have told this story without her love, understanding, and help. It is also dedicated to our daughter Melissa who has brought a whole new meaning to life for us.

As a novice author who decided to self-publish, it wasn't long before I realized how much I didn't know about what I was doing. At every step I've been amazed to find people willing to help me through the process. Many of them have been family and friends – but there have also been complete strangers I've met along the way that lent a helping hand. Some of them have made significant contributions of their time and knowledge in research, photography, and editing what I have written. Even though I decided to self-publish, I have come to realize I couldn't have done it by myself. I hope to remember each with an autographed copy of my book expressing my gratitude for their effort that was so generously given.

I would also like to thank everyone that takes the time to read this book. Because I am self-published, the success of this book is very much reliant on your word-of-mouth referrals to others. If you would like to follow my blog, leave a comment, order a book, or pass the information on to others that might be interested, you will find me at

www.MotorcyclesPlanesandRevolution.com

Woodworking plane with author's mark,
photo courtesy of Bob Poull and Paul Moroder

Table Of Contents

Author & daughter riding Harley-Davidson
4th of July parade 2005

A Biker's Prayer

Bless me on my trip today and keep me safe in your care. Help me to notice all
the little things along the way that I should have the common sense to avoid.
Sharpen my senses, not only for a safe journey – but also to the enjoyment of all that
surrounds me. Help me to care for those that accompany me and those that I meet
along the way. Help me to keep a clear head and remain calm even if I am oppressed.
In the end, please return me home refreshed and filled with the freedom and beauty
that you have provided for my enjoyment this fine day.

by Michael J. Hanley

1   Overture to Celebrate Freedom

I ride Harley-Davidson. For me riding is not just a hobby, it is an incredible part of life. On a beautiful day there are few things more important than riding. On nice days only the most serious responsibilities are met so there is time left for a ride. When the weather is nice you don't want to be caught doing something foolish like cutting the lawn. My neighbor rides John Deere – I ride Harley-Davidson.

I live in Wisconsin where the winters are cold and bleak. Some folks are depressed by the cold short days and lack of sunlight. This illness is real and the prescription is to find more light – either sitting on the beach in Florida or under special light bulbs at home. I'm not troubled by this – my illness is riding, and I've got it bad. The fact I can't ride in winter is depressing enough to make me think about moving to a warmer climate. They say that global warming has shortened the winter at the North Pole, melting the ice and affecting the polar bears. Perhaps this is so, but I have not seen it warm the frozen tundra here in Wisconsin to extend my riding season, and to me that would be a real benefit to counter this thorny debate.

I feel like I've ridden forever. I started riding early as a kid on my bicycle. By age 13 I was out around the countryside bicycling 60 miles with a friend to his uncle's farm. We camped for two weeks in a pasture by a stream. We had it all – or really I should say we brought it all along. I had an old Columbia 2 speed bike with fat whitewall tires that looked sort of like the Harley I ride today. This bicycle was built like a '57 Chevy – not one of the svelte 20 speed titanium rimmed jobs we buy now. I had my Boy Scout pack with clothes and cooking gear, a canvass pup tent, canteen, my dad's army shovel – probably over 100 pounds of gear strapped on the back. We pushed the bikes up most hills because they were so heavy, so I'm not sure if it really qualified as a ride. It took us 12 hours to reach our destination, but what a trip.

When I think about it – that was only about 5 miles per hour and not much faster than walking – but there was this incredible sense of freedom. We were out of the city in the open air, did our own cooking, watermelon chilling in the stream, campfires to warm us at night. Through the Boy Scouts I was already hunter certified and an NRA rated sharpshooter, and we got to do some shooting out on the farm. Even though I had asthma pretty bad, we helped the farmer with haying – real work and not just delivering newspapers. If all that wasn't enough, the farmer had a daughter and some friends that we hung around with. We were absolutely on our own at age 13 – what a trip.

For us this was the very definition of freedom and the meaning of life – and the bikes made it possible. So we worked another year and used our paper route money to buy new

Schwinn 5 speeds. We lightened up on our camp gear – and we did it again. Eventually we got it down to a 6 hour trip and let me tell you, no more walking bikes up hills! We were up to an average 10 mph.

Figure 1: Author's first motorcycle, Honda 305 Superhawk in 1967

When it came time to get my license a car really never was an option. We were on the lower end of middle class and my family couldn't afford a second car for my mother even though she worked full time. At the time you could buy a small used motorcycle for a couple hundred dollars – and it got 4-5 times better gas mileage then a car. I had already been riding for years and I loved it – this was just a bit faster (there's a trend here). Buying a motorcycle was probably the easiest decision I've ever made in my life, and I've never looked back.

I guess it's hard to explain this passion for riding a motorcycle – it seems bikers are not so easy to understand. When I started riding in the 60's bikers were not an accepted part of society. My first cycle was a Honda 305cc Superhawk (shown above). I was clean shaven and college bound and probably looked like something out of a Beach Boys song. Even though I wasn't wearing leathers back then, there were a couple of times someone in a car purposely tried to run me off the road. Some of that old stigma continues to haunt bikers today, but times have changed and motorcycle riding has gone mainstream just as it was prior to WWII. Today most folks realize this is not a small section of society leading a deviant lifestyle. Today almost anyone you know could be a biker, and we've learned to live with the fact that even the president can lead a deviant lifestyle. Ironically, even though I'm in sales and meet with management of billion dollar companies, I probably look more deviant today riding my Harley then I did back in college when folks perceived me as bad just because I was on a motorcycle — regardless of how straight I looked. Still, if folks are more accepting of bikers today, I'm not sure they understand why we love to ride.

There is this incredible sense of freedom when you are riding with the wind in your face and hair. There is the warmth of the sunshine on your back and the trees and fields create a feast for your eyes. You immediately feel the coolness when the sun goes behind a cloud or the extra warmth when you ride out of a shaded area of trees along the road. And, oh YES there is the speed — accelerating to 65mph on a motorcycle is not the same as in a car! On a cycle every sense is heightened and every muscle in your body works with the machine to complete each move. Your mind and reflexes must be totally engaged. The engine is right there between your legs, up close and personal. You feel the road, literally. When I go over a hill and look down I often feel a rush of adrenalin, and the curves are to die for.

You may think you can experience this rush with a great home theatre, going to the IMAX, riding a roller coaster, or sitting in one of those machines at the mall that gives you "the total experience" of something. But there are very few things you can do in life that really match the experience of riding a motorcycle. You could take up horseback riding, flying an ultra light plane, mountain climbing, skydiving, sailboating, surfboarding, or diving off a reef swimming with the sharks. None of these are daily activities for most of us, and most are even more expensive then motorcycles. It is sad that many of us think we experience life to its fullest sitting in the cocoon of our car. I once got a hint of the riding experience driving a convertible over the San Francisco Bay Bridge. I remember feeling "wow – I'm right out here in the open – no protection". But to really get the riding experience you'd have to remove the hood, move the steering wheel up front, and drive the car while sitting on the engine. Try to imagine crossing the Bay Bridge doing that!

The freedom of riding goes well beyond the senses because you are actually going somewhere, getting away from it all. As a youth this was my freedom to be somewhere else away from my family, siblings, and all that. Because of the heightened senses and emotions, riding is an escape from life in general, the boss, and all the crap at work. If the sun is shining just call me Hellen Gone! This is similar to the escape to go hunting or fishing, hiking in the mountains and other activities that people are passionate about. Jean Davidson relates that the founders of Harley-Davidson loved fishing, and it was in part their desire to get away for a little fishing that prompted them to build their first motorcycle.[1]

In 1972 I was just out of college and just married. My wife Dee and I loaded up our BMW 650 and headed off to see Colorado. We bought compact lightweight camping gear and packed it on the cycle for the trip. The bedrolls were strapped on top of the saddlebags – and that same trusty Boy Scout knapsack on the rack behind. This created a relatively spartan "easy chair" for Dee, and she wrote postcards on my back as we rode down I-80. The temps hit 104 and you could actually see the heat coming off the pavement in waves as we passed through Nebraska. Finally we reached the foot of the Big Thompson Canyon and rode in wonder up the mountains to Estes Park. We pulled into the campground late that evening with campfires all around and someone was playing the flute. We thought we had ridden into the outskirts of heaven.

Figure 2: Author and wife with BMW R60/5 in 1972

We spent the next three weeks riding the Rocky Mountains – the roads are breathtaking. The height of our trip (literally) was biking up Old Fall River Road, the original road over the Continental Divide following the old Indian hunting trails. This is a one lane unpaved

1   *Growing up Harley-Davidson*, by Jean Davidson, granddaughter of the founder Walter Davidson

road going one-way up the mountain, and even in mid-June it had just been cleared with 4-6' snowdrifts alongside the road. We ate our bag lunch at 12,000 feet on top of the mountain and rode back down Trail Ridge Road, the highest continuous paved road in the United States. Anyone can enjoy this spectacular view riding in a car, but it is so different out there in the open air on two wheels, your body leaning into the curves of each cutback, the mountain walls rising up on your left and a 6,000 ft drop-off on the right. Talk about Rocky Mountain High – no drugs necessary!

I realize not everyone rides a cycle or even wants to, so maybe it's hard to relate to this feeling of freedom. Perhaps you have gone hiking, camping, fishing or golfing – or perhaps you know someone close to you that is passionate about these activities? Perhaps you can remember your first bicycle or your first car and that feeling of freedom that rushed over you at the time?

Figure 3: Author's Harley-Davidson at a Wisconsin rally in 2005

There is a particular ride I enjoy a short distance from my home to one of Wisconsin's beautiful lake towns, and I ride it often. Someone once asked me if I ride for the ride alone – or is it about the destination? This is the quintessential question of life – is it important how you live it or is it just where you go in the end? Bikers will tell you it is the ride. If there is a fun destination, well that's OK too – but the magic is in the ride itself. My ride to Lake Geneva is like that. I'm gone 60-90 min if that's all the time I can spare. The road has some hills and curves – lots of fields and trees to enjoy as the seasons pass me by. Lately it seems they go by almost as fast as the trees. There is the sun and the clouds, and yes Lake Geneva is a fun stop as well. Maybe there is time for a cup of coffee, walk around the shops a bit, bring home a good loaf of bread for dinner, and sometimes a bottle of wine. If that isn't enough (and it never is) I still have the ride home!

Often I get this sliver of time to ride late in the afternoon. In autumn as the days shorten, by the time I ride home the sun is spent and low on the horizon. The entrance to the road home pulls uphill sharply and I accelerate hard, leaning into a beautiful curve just as I break the crest of the hill. For just a moment there is this thrill – the view into the valley below looking down on the trees and crops. The wind and the engine are screaming in my ears but the peace of this moment is complete. The sun has caught the clouds on fire and is still just strong enough to warm the ride. It is in this moment when I am at one with the cycle and with nature that I realize – yes, this is how it is supposed to be – this is how God meant it to be.

There is a road like this just outside of Boston that I hope to ride someday. There is a story about a particular spring morning when Francis Smith was riding his horse along this road. People that ride horses have much in common with bikers – the whole body is involved riding a horse and we have a common love of leather. We are equally passionate about our ride, although horses don't have the high speed or the rumbling sound of the engine as part of their experience. Horse riders and bikers might disagree on the essential need for these. For both riders nature is up close and personal – you can reach out and touch a leaf on a tree branch as they are sometimes that close. In this story, Francis Smith rode his horse, breaking the crest of a hill just as the sun was rising to burn off the fog and warm the day. Perhaps the clouds were on fire that morning too as the sun rose in the sky, reminiscent of the clouds of smoke and volleys of fire just spent on a small group of troublemakers encountered down on Lexington Common[2]. The year was 1775 and on the morning of April 19th Lieut. Col Francis Smith led a column of the King's troops out of Lexington. As he looked down into the small valley below on the road to Concord, I should guess he had that same momentary thrill. "Yes, this is how it is supposed to be – this is how God meant it to be." However, Lieut. Col Francis Smith was lucky to live through the day as Americans took up arms to fight for our freedom in the first battle of the American Revolution.

I would like to share with you a story about the beginning of our Revolution. Other wars have been perpetrated by Kings and politicians and often fought by armies with little understanding of why, but our Revolution was led and fought by individuals who chose to fight because of strong personal feelings about how to live their lives. I would like to introduce you to some of these common people and ask 'what were they thinking' as each of them made their own decision to take up arms and put their life on the line. Most of them played their role without the experience necessary to fight the most powerful army on earth, much less to create a new nation as had never been done before. If you step back and think about it the story has almost miraculous qualities to it. I realize that some of us don't like reading history, so I've cast the history more in the form of a story and you will NOT find a test anywhere on names and dates at the end of each chapter. So if you'll allow me some leeway, let's begin.

---

2   The town Common or "green" surrounded by the church and other buildings as the town was first laid out.

2   First Movement

After the Battle of Lexington and Concord, there were folks on both sides who thought it might have been an aberration – an event spun out of control. There was plenty of confusion to go around as the King's troops marched onto Lexington Common early that morning. The men of Lexington standing on the common numbered too few, and to fire first would have been a mistake more akin to suicide. If the British fired first, the rest of the day's fighting by the colonials might be chalked up to emotions run amuck over their men killed and wounded in Lexington those first few minutes. However, the fight that happened in Lexington and Concord the day of April 19th in 1775 had been boiling for years, and the Battle of Bunker Hill just two months later would make it clear this was no aberration.

Nine years earlier Parliament had passed a string of Stamp Acts to collect taxes - which the colonies bitterly opposed. Seeing very little tax revenue, Parliament passed the Military Act which placed the cost and burden of housing the King's troops directly on to private citizens in their homes. We can imagine how well that went over. Citizens taunting the King's troops quartered in the city prompted them to open fire on the crowd, resulting in the Boston Massacre. Courts and judges set up by each town were then ordered disbanded – to be replaced by judges appointed by the Crown – and those arrested could be drug off to England for a "fair trial". The judges appointed by the Crown were threatened with mayhem, and never took office. The next Stamp Act was on tea sold in the Americas and resulted in the Boston Tea Party with colonists dressed as Indians throwing an entire load of tea into Boston harbor.

We Americans love the story of the Boston Tea Party, but really now, let's take a look at this from the British point of view. The Crown had a legitimate right to tax at home and in all its colonies around the world. Because they objected to "taxation without representation", the reaction in Boston was for a group of educated men to appear in greasepaint and commit breaking and entering, grand theft, and destruction of the King's property. The Crown probably felt this was a bit excessive and they should have all been thrown in prison. But talk about excessive; Parliament retaliated by shutting down the port of Boston. How exactly do you do that to a port and a whole city you might ask? They simply moved the Royal Customs House north a bit to Salem and stopped all shipping traffic in Boston harbor compliments of the Royal Navy.

Through the bleak winter of 1774-75 the King's troops occupied the city while British warships essentially blockaded the port of Boston. By any reasoning was this not an act of war? By any measure these were severe times: businessmen were ruined and people in Boston were brought to the point of starvation. Meanwhile, the British commander was well aware of troubling events in the countryside surrounding Boston. There was the Continental Congress appointing Committees of Safety, supplies being gathered, and Minutemen drilling in most every town. You can almost hear folks saying to the British commander "well, you can't just sit here with all this going on". So it was with winter gone by in April the British decided to send troops up to Lexington to possibly capture the "troublemakers" John Hancock and Samuel Adams – and thence to Concord to capture a horde of powder and other supplies being collected there.[3]

The colonists were also aware of the goings-on inside Boston. The British army had already made a few day trips to the surrounding countryside, and it was hard to misread the movement of troops in tight city streets. Thus it was that Paul Revere and the Sons of Liberty (here's a real group of troublemakers) made plans to warn the countryside when movement was afoot. Paul Revere was not the only rider to spread the warning around the countryside the night of April 18th, but his ride took him directly to Lexington and is certainly the one most remembered. Without this warning, the events of the next day would certainly have been quite different.

The British force gathered at the foot of Boston Common and then boarded the Navy's longboats about 10:30 that night. The force of about 800 men crossed the Charles River and landed in East Cambridge in a marsh. Ferrying across the river was a slow process and several trips were required, so the force was not completely assembled on the Cambridge shore and ready to move until 1:00 in the morning. The confidence of the British officers in their ability to complete the assigned task without any serious challenge showed in their decision to issue just 36 rounds of ammunition to each soldier.[4]

Figure 4: Painting depicting the midnight ride of Paul Revere by A.L. Ripley in 1937, courtesy of the National Archives and Records Administration

Paul Revere and the handful of other riders that came out of Boston on their "midnight ride" were well ahead of the British force that night, and they set off a network of riders reaching as far as Worchester 40 miles west of Boston before noon. By now the British also knew any hope of surprise was lost by the warning shots they'd heard in the night, so they sent back for reinforcements and pressed their march on to Lexington. The men of Lexington were warned the British were coming and indeed Hancock and Adams made their escape. However, Lexington's early scouts reported no sign of the British column, so in the middle of the night there was confusion about how close the danger was.

---

3   *The Battle of April 19 1775* by Frank Warren Coburn, p17. I reference Coburn extensively and enjoyed reading his book as background for my brief portrayal of the battle here.
4   Ibid p19, 20

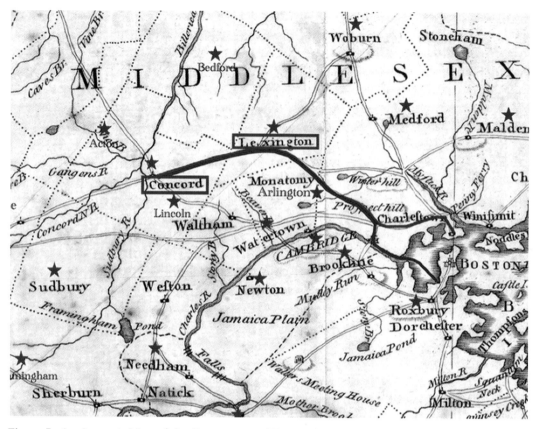

Figure 5: An Accurate Map of the Country round Boston in New England by Archibald Hamilton in 1776, engraved for the Town & Country Magazine in London 1776, courtesy American Geographical Society Library, University of Wisconsin-Milwaukee Libraries. Artwork courtesy of Debra Wahlers

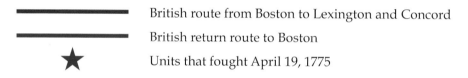

British route from Boston to Lexington and Concord

British return route to Boston

★   Units that fought April 19, 1775

Only when the British column was on the outskirts of town did Lexington get reports of its actual sighting. Capt. John Parker of Lexington immediately ordered his drummer to beat to arms. The initial line that formed was just 38 men, but then quickly grew to about 65.[5] Capt. Parker instructed his Minutemen "Let the troops pass by and don't molest them without they begin first".[6] This was prudent, because Parker's men were only about half assembled as the British entered town. It was early, about 5:00 in the morning and Revere's warning had not yet brought support from nearby towns who may have been worried about being attacked themselves. Besides, recent confrontations with the British army had all ended with the British backing off without shots fired by either side. So neither side expected what happened next.

5   *The Battle of April 19 1775* by Frank Warren Coburn, p62
6   Ibid p31

The advance column of British light infantry were not in plain sight until the last moment as they turned the corner and marched onto Lexington Common 300-400 strong. As the direct representative of the King of England they presented an overwhelming show of force with their flags flying and three mounted officers at their head. This company directly represented the full power of the King of England. Capt. Parker's meager force of 65 men stood the Common directly blocking the British advance, and he initially commanded his men "stand their ground" but not to fire first. Can we imagine the courage it took for this small group of rabble to stand their ground for even a moment? Still, seeing the hopelessness of their situation, Parker then ordered the men to disperse or fall back, but he did not order his men to surrender their arms as the British demanded. At this point as the Minutemen fell back, a single shot (who knows whose) prompted the British commander to order his troops to fire. The ensuing charge left eight American men dead and nine wounded, including "Prince Estabrook, a man of color".[7] One of every four men that stood the Common for Lexington was dead or wounded. The fighting was up-close and personal. Sons stood to arms next to their fathers and wives held their dying men in their arms. The entire British force now back together gave huzzas and marched on to Concord unscathed. All of this happened in the course of about 30 minutes.

★   ★   ★   ★   ★

The British column reached Concord without incident about 8:00 in the morning. One company of Concord Minutemen stood the road at the outskirts of town, and then turned and marched into Concord with their own drums and fifes playing while the British followed behind – what a sight that must have been.[8] We should be clear that the Committee of Safety had indeed been collecting military stores at Concord that were considered contraband by the Crown. "Within the town (of Concord) scattered through the cellars and attics and outbuildings…of at least twenty-five houses, the provincials had concealed ten tons of musket balls and cartridges, thirty-five half barrels of powder, 350 tents, foodstuffs, …and a substantial number of cannon and gun carriages".[9] The British commander now split his force - sending portions to the north and south bridge - with the main force ordered to locate the cache of military supplies he was sent to destroy.

News of the deaths at Lexington had spread like wildfire and reached Concord even before the British troops arrived. Something else arrived in Concord before the British – Minutemen from a number of surrounding towns came with a heightened sense of the events at hand. These men were roused hours earlier and now had clear reports of where the British were headed and where they needed to be. In the hills surrounding Concord

---

7   *The Battle of April 19 1775* by Frank Warren Coburn, p70
8   Ibid p74
9   *The Minutemen the First Fight: Myths and Realities of the American Revolution*, by John R. Galvin, p140

there were now almost 500 Minutemen and Militia[10] and the makings of a real fight were at hand, one very different from the beating suffered at Lexington.

Figure 6: Minuteman Statue at Concord Mass, picture courtesy of National Park Service

Like the men of Lexington, the men of Concord did not directly confront the British, and strategically withdrew to high ground north of town to watch and decide a course of action with their neighboring townsmen. Even as the gathered officers held a council of war, smoke rose from the fires of contraband material being destroyed in Concord. This was easily mistaken for the British having put the town to the torch, and the council promptly decided to confront the British and put an end to this. The colonial men that began their march back into Concord came directly up against the British stationed to guard the north bridge – and thus the fight began. The British fired first. Regardless if they were warning shots or not, this time with Lexington on their mind, the British volley was instantly answered with real shots effectively aimed. While both sides took some casualties, a number of British officers were hit and their force retreated from the bridge. This was the first direct attack against the British by colonial troops and clearly an act of treason by the Crown's measure.

By the rude bridge that arched the flood,
Their flag to April's breeze unfurled,
Here once the embattled farmers stood,
And fired the shot heard round the world.[11]

Their work done in Concord by about 10:00am, the British commander decided to rest his men before ordering the return trip to Boston. His men had little or no sleep the night before and many had stood hours in the marsh at Cambridge. The shortest distance any of them had marched was 17 miles – some quite a bit more. They had been involved in two skirmishes and now had casualties to contend with. Most important, he had sent a request for reinforcements prior to Lexington as he realized they'd lost the element of surprise. Now as they sensed the gathering "rabble" around them, he hoped the reinforcements might be close at hand.

10 *The Battle of April 19 1775* by Frank Warren Coburn, p 81
11 *Concord Hymn* by Ralph Waldo Emerson

It was noon before the order was given to march on the return to Boston. All the while as the British rested, Minutemen poured in from surrounding towns. The column of 800 British soldiers now faced a combined force of 1,500 Americans. The town of Reading alone had sent four companies with a total of 291 men that joined the fight just south of Concord. One of the Reading companies was led by Capt. John Walton who was 65 years of age[12] and marched 18 miles to reach Concord – a distance equal to what the British had marched. We'll learn more about John Walton in a later chapter.

Now began a long and fearsome gauntlet as the British column retreated to Boston. They no longer held the advantage of numbers and the patriots knew exactly where they were headed. While the British were confined to the road with little or no cover, the patriots used the hills, trees, and rocks surrounding the road for cover as they had learned in the French and Indian wars. For their part, the British discipline held up and they made good use of flanking units through the woods to inflict casualties on the patriots. The patriots were acting as individual units – sometimes individual men – and there was no central commander to take maximum advantage of the situation – or the British may well have been destroyed instead of just taking heavy casualties.

As the British column returned to Lexington they once again met Capt Parker's Lexington Company's full complement of 120 Minutemen as they re-joined the fight. The British no longer enjoyed the overwhelming show of force presented on their first visit to Lexington. Lieut. Col. Francis Smith was forced to fight his way back up the hill where he had sat on his horse earlier that morning so sure of himself, feeling that all was well with the world. Now his ranks were broken and disordered – riddled with wounded including Smith himself. Many had been killed or fallen exhausted by the wayside. Now too, the confident British ration of just 36 rounds per soldier began to run out.

It was fully 3:00 in the afternoon and the other side of Lexington before the British column fell exhausted inside the protection of their reinforcements.[13] An officer described them "as lying prone on the ground, like dogs with protruding tongues".[14] The British fired up the road with two cannon to scatter the Americans and hold them off long enough to re-group. Now as they halted, the British began looting and burning homes and barns on a scale large enough to believe their commander must have ordered it. The British retreat to Cambridge was effective if still harassed, but wanton destruction and killing of the old and infirm are their legacy.

---

12 The Battle of April 19 1775 by Frank Warren Coburn , p96- 97
13 Ibid p111
14 History of the Origin, Progress, and Termination of the American War, by C. Steadman, London 1794

★　★　★　★　★

The British column reached Charlestown as the sun set, never to rise again on Middlesex County under the rule of the British Crown.[15] As evening fell the British had a combined force of 1,500 soldiers facing a growing American force of almost 3,800 men.[16] If it had been possible to gain control of this superior force the Americans could have prevented the British from ever reaching Charlestown. Ironically, the British camped that night on Bunker Hill. Little could they know the terrible cost of re-claiming this same hill as they abandoned it the next day and returned to Boston.

From every point of view the Battle of Lexington and Concord was a seismic event – it really was the shot heard round the world! The British army was the most powerful in the world, and they suffered a humiliating loss with three times the American casualties. Many of the American fighters were youngsters and old men. The British regulars were beaten by what they regarded as common rabble in front of many onlookers in broad daylight. Lord Percy is quoted later as saying "I never believed, I confess, that they would have attacked the King's troops…. Whoever dares to look upon them as an irregular mob will find himself much mistaken. They have men among them who know very well what they are about"[17]

By the next morning the number of Massachusetts Minutemen and Militia had grown to something like 20,000 men who commenced the siege of Boston. This was about equal to the whole population of Boston including the meager force of 5,000 British soldiers occupying the city. Can you imagine? By today's measure this would be something like 600,000 men showing up on the outskirts of Boston. This massing of force was done without phones or e-mail, without cars, trucks, motorcycles or even horses and wagons. For the most part these men marched to Boston armed and ready to fight in the span of about 24 hours. This fact alone, ignoring the battle and the outcome, is just incredible. I wonder if our National Guard could accomplish a similar feat today? Like Robert Redford and Paul Newman in Butch Cassidy and the Sundance Kid, I should guess as General Gage awoke that next morning in Boston and looked out his window at the horizon, he may have asked wistfully "Who are all those guys?"

---

15 *The Battle of April 19 1775* by Frank Warren Coburn, p154
16 Ibid, p133, 161
17 *Minute Man* brochure, National Park Service, Dep't of the Interior

"The first blow for liberty". Print by A.H. Ritchie.
Courtesy of the National Archives and Records Administration

3 A Cast of Common Men

Thus far we have talked about motorcycles, the American Revolution, and freedom. Perhaps you have wondered how planes fit into our story when the Wright brothers didn't learn to fly until 1903 – coincidentally the very same year William Harley and the brothers Davidson crafted their first. Certainly 1903 was a banner year for Yankee ingenuity! However, the planes in my story are the lowly handplanes used by the housewrights and woodworkers of colonial times.

There were only a small number of men that made planes here in the colonies the last half of the 1700's – real men that made handplanes as part of their living and also happened to fight in the Revolution to win our freedom. None of these men planned this role in life – they were simply in the right place at the right time and did what they felt must be done. None of them was any more noteworthy than you or I, and ironically each would have been forgotten in time if it were not for the planes they made that have survived for us today.

Figure 7: Author hand planning a raised panel for a door, photo by Bob Poull

When we tour an historic home and look at the fine architectural details and furniture, we tend to focus on who lived there and what their life was like. Seldom do we think about the artisans who did this work or the kit of tools they used to create such artistry they left for us to enjoy. We don't think much about the importance of handplanes to life in early America – but they were important indeed. Prior to the handplane, the working of wood into finished products like doors, window frames, raised paneled wainscot, fireplace mantles, and furniture was all done by a highly specialized craftsman with nothing more than a few chisels. This meant the cost was very high, so only nobility and the very rich had access to such comforts. The rest of us common folk were consigned to rough hewn tables with a stool or half-log to sit on and most likely no windows in our humble living space. The crude door would have kept out intruders, but not the cold winds of North American winters. The humble plane made working wood much easier, higher quality, and substantially faster. More trained craftsmen also helped bring prices down, making such comforts available even for the common man. Quite literally these planes were The Powertools of the 1700's!

Today handplanes are the common stuff of flea markets just as the men we'll meet were common men, the basic working class of the 1700s. However, the planes they left us cannot be called common, for they are rare in today's market and some are beautiful to the point of being art. I have been lucky enough to find some of these planes – some quite by accident and others deliberately as I learned more about them. Ultimately these planes brought me to ask, just like General Gage, who were these men? They led me to learn more about the Revolution and the roles they played, and to think about the meaning of this freedom they won for us.

Figure 8: New England planes of the 1700s, author's collection, photo by Bob Poull

Beginning in 1620, there was a migration of people to the Massachusetts Bay Colony, and for the most part they couldn't bring bulky items like doors or furniture on the boat with them. Besides, lumber was in short supply in England. As a result, craftsmen and their tools were in great demand in the new colony as they built homes, town meeting halls, and furniture of our native woods that were so abundant across the colony. However, the tools they used were most definitely NOT supposed to be made in the Massachusetts Bay Colony.

The Americas, like any colony, were a means of building an empire for England. Colonies were to provide a cheap source of raw material such as lumber, tobacco, and eventually cotton to supply England's industrial revolution. In return, the colonies must buy the goods produced in England, keeping the British businessmen and economy healthy and securing plenty of jobs for the British citizens. Tools were near the top of the list of products made in England. If the British economy were to remain strong, it wouldn't do for the colonies to create their own industrial capability, depriving England of both the cheap natural resources they needed and the market to sell their wares. To prevent this, English Mercantile laws of the time actually prohibited certain artisans like toolmakers from leaving England for fear that valuable expertise would reach the colonies and eventually become a competitor to England. In spite of those laws, we know of a planemaker born and trained in Scotland by the name of Thomas Napier who landed in the city of Philadelphia in November of 1774 on the very eve of the Revolution. On leaving England, Thomas Napier falsified his papers stating his trade as "farmer" and providing a false hometown that he knew from his youth.[18] Even still, it is amazing how well the mercantile system worked for England as they dominated American tool making well past the War of 1812. It is interesting to note how England protected their jobs and economy, in comparison to how the United States most recently allowed our jobs to be sent almost anywhere in the world.

Because of these Mercantile laws, mid 1700's commercial centers like Boston had almost no planemakers due to the ready supply of English tools at a fair price – and in Boston you were always under the watchful eye of the Mother Country. However, as settlers moved inland and built smaller towns this control broke down, and a small group of planemakers plied their trade with the town of Wrentham, Massachusetts at the center of this basically illicit activity (more troublemakers – there's a trend here too). In a way, these handplanes made in Wrentham symbolize "the secret weapon" that won the American Revolution. These planes were among the first signs of men showing independence in their thinking that permeated their religious, economic, and ultimately their political endeavors. After all, if enough people decide they will live life as they choose rather than how they are told, this is the very definition of revolution.

From 1728 to 1753, a man named Francis Nicholson made planes as his primary living in Wrentham, Mass. Francis is generally recognized as the father of American planemaking. Wrentham was a sleepy little town in 1750 – as it is today - pretty much in the middle of nowhere. However, Francis chose Wrentham because it was on the Post Road a bit over half way from Boston to Providence, and thence on to New York. Francis set up his shop right on this highway – the 1750 equivalent of e-commerce on the information superhighway.

Figure 9: Planes with makers mark on front toe, author's collection, photo by Bob Poull

We know all this because of a fortunate practice of the times. Many planemakers, Francis included, marked the front end or "toe" of their planes with their name and often where they lived and worked. We may think of a planemaker marking his work as advertising pure and simple. Francis didn't need to mark his planes LIVING* IN WRENTHAM to impress his neighbors. He marked the planes to let woodworkers and merchants up and down the Post Road know how to find him so he could sell more planes. Who could have foretold that these same marks stamped on their planes would help modern researchers find these men 200 years after they disappeared like the shavings under their bench, lost to history? These handplanes are relatively unique as items made in the colonial period marked with their makers' names - that allow us an insight to these common men of the period.

---

18 *Tho Napier – The Scottish Connection* by Alan G Bates p19, 20

Francis Nicholson was a key figure in his church and town and quite a story in his own rite. His son John worked for him, as did a Negro slave named Cesar Chelor. When Francis died he gave Cesar Chelor his freedom along with a piece of his land and tools, and Chelor continued making planes under his own name for another 30 years as a respected member of the Wrentham community[19]. All three of these makers were too old to fight in the Revolution, are already well documented and not the primary focus of my story. There was, however, another family of woodworkers who made planes in Wrentham that has remained unknown until now, and one of them did answer the call to arms for our American Revolution.

★ ★ ★ ★ ★

Noah Pratt was a yeoman (landowner-farmer), housewright, joiner (furniture maker), and eventually referred to as a gentleman according to various legal documents of his time. On April 19th in 1775 Noah Pratt responded to the call at Lexington and Concord as a sergeant in a Minuteman company for Wrentham where he and his family made their home. Wrentham sent eight companies in response to the Lexington alarm totaling approximately 320 of their best men. Noah's place in history is marked on the muster roll of his company of 42 men sworn by Capt. Oliver Pond[20], his commander and his closest neighbor to the north.

We have no idea how long it took the alarm cast by Paul Revere into the Massachusetts countryside to ripple out and reach Wrentham. Mapquest.com says Wrentham is 34 miles from Charlestown where Revere began his ride, and today we can do it in just 47 minutes. However, Noah's company covered the 34 miles walking with a pack and rifle. This might have taken 8-10 hours once they received the alarm. The map on the next page shows Minuteman units from the area around Boston that actually fought on April 19th, and nobody anywhere near Wrentham arrived at the battle before the British fell exhausted into Charlestown that night. However, Noah's unit likely made it to the outskirts of Boston by nightfall, and he served a total of 11 days opening the siege of Boston and the Revolutionary War itself. Noah Pratt was one of the 20,000 men surrounding Gen. Gage the morning after Lexington and Concord. Let's try to answer Gen. Gage's question of "who were all these men" – by learning something more about Noah Pratt.

---

19 Cesar Chelor and the World He Lived In by Richard T. DeAvilla
20 Massachusetts Soldiers and Sailors of the Revolution, p708

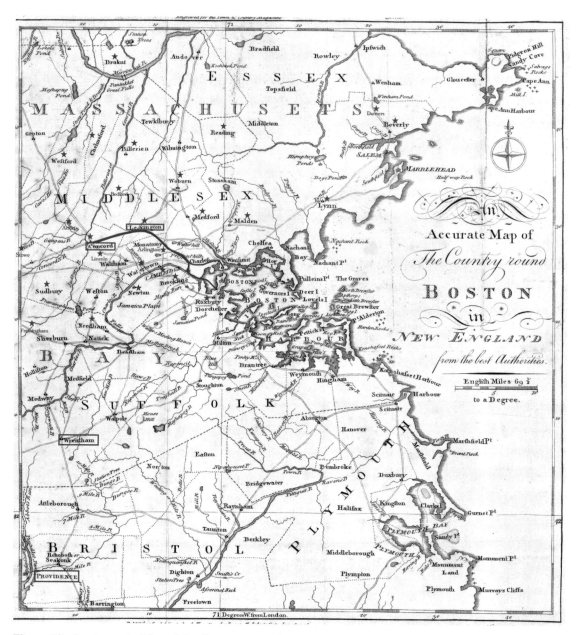

Figure 10: An Accurate Map of the Country round Boston in New England by Archibald Hamilton in 1776, engraved for the Town & Country Magazine in London 1776, courtesy American Geographical Society Library, University of Wisconsin-Milwaukee Libraries. Artwork courtesy of Debra Wahlers

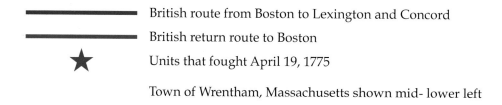

British route from Boston to Lexington and Concord

British return route to Boston

Units that fought April 19, 1775

Town of Wrentham, Massachusetts shown mid- lower left

Noah was a farmer with a home and 48 acres between what is now Dedham St and East St - near the intersection of Thurston St[21] less than a mile from Wrentham meeting house. The men of each Minuteman Company decided who would lead them into battle – so as a sergeant we know that Noah held the respect of his neighbors. This is noteworthy considering Noah was born in Newton, Mass[22] and doesn't appear in Wrentham records until just five years before the war when he married a young lady named Hannah Sterns in 1770. By the Battle of Lexington and Concord, Noah and Hannah Pratt had two sons named Henry and Nathan. In this short time Noah Pratt was one of the guys, well liked, and someone they felt you could count on in a pinch.

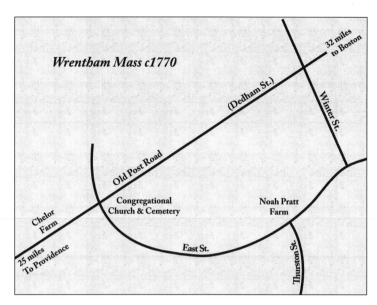

Figure 11: Noah Pratt lived just 1 mile from Wrentham Meeting House and less than 2 miles from Cesar Chelor, drawing by Debra Wahlers

In 1774 legal documents Noah Pratt is referred to as a housewright in Wrentham.[23] In fact, Noah is descended from Phinehas Pratt who arrived on the Sparrow in 1622 near Plymouth with the second group of Pilgrims. Phinehas was also a joiner, and "the house which he built was two stories high, with a gable roof: the lower story was of stone: and the upper portion of wood. The windows were of a small diamond pattern of glass "quarrels" inserted in leaden sashes".[24] The home that Phinehas built sounds like quite a home for early Massachusetts. Noah Pratt came from sound stock and a solid tradition of woodworking.

Figure 12: Timberframed home

Building a home in the 1700s meant timberframing, a method of joining large timbers with furniture-like joints to build the structure. The PBS series *This Old House* re-introduced this form of construction to viewers with a timberframed home built by Ted Benson

---

21 Suffolk Cty land records 174-197 sale to Dr Jankes Norton filled in 1792.
22 Mormons, Noah Pratt born 3-5-1748 in Newton, Mass of father Oliver Pratt (b 1710 Needham d 5-17-1763 in Newton), mother Sarah Willard (b 1726)
23 Suffolk Cty probate dated May 27, 1774 docket #15640 with special thanks to Sue Bacheller
24 Phinehas Pratt's Descendents 1622-1987 by Priscilla Lorena Pratt Briggs

Figure 13: Author (in blue) and friend Bob Poull raise a post timber that is 8x8x11ft tall. Note the mortise at top of post ready to hold the beam that will set on it.

in the 1980s and another more recently. As a woodworker, I timberframed portions of my own home and studio – and I can tell you this is hard work even today. As a housewright Noah was a man among men. He could move a 400-pound oak timber fourteen foot long and make it look easy – he could do it all day long. Moreover, he was educated in the art of woodworking and joinery, the geometry of laying out a house square and true, and the physics of moving and lifting massive weight without killing himself or his friends. It was also part of Noah's life to lead the homeowner's family and neighbors in lifting the framed sections of the home into place on raising day. If you want to catch my drift here you should watch the movie *Witness* with Harrison Ford and Kelly McGillis - a superb use of modern cinematography showing an Amish timberframed barn being raised!

Like most of the citizens of Wrentham, Noah was a Puritan – which we will explore in more detail in a bit. As shown on the map previous page, Noah lived within a couple of miles of Cesar Chelor (the black planemaker in Wrentham) and most certainly attended church 'meeting' with him on a weekly basis for the better part of fourteen years until Chelor's death. There is no question these two men knew each other over an extended period of time. As a freeman and a respected member of the church, Cesar Chelor voted right alongside Noah Pratt as the people of Wrentham decided their fate going into the Revolutionary War.

Like Cesar Chelor, Noah Pratt also made planes - at least for himself in his own work. Here is a picture of a fine 18th century crown moulding plane made of cherry wood marked N*P that I believe was made and used by Noah Pratt in his own work while living in Wrentham. You can see that Noah had an eye for fine woodworking details in his interior

Figure 14: Crown moulding plane by Noah Pratt c1776, author's collection, photo by Bob Poull

trim and furniture. Noah's oldest son Henry also made planes and went on to be one of America's earliest organ makers using skills learned at his father's bench in Wrentham.

In 1792 Noah Pratt had the confidence to pack up his entire family and move them 100 miles to Winchester, NH and build a new life. In his journal, Noah's grandson Addison Pratt recalled "I have heard it observed by my Grandmother Pratt (Noah's wife Hannah) that a dog and gun is the regalia of the Pratt's, and I think that a fishhook might be added…".[25]

So, let's answer Gen. Gage's question about "who were all those men" massed outside Boston the morning after Lexington and Concord. Noah Pratt was one of them, a sergeant in his company of Minutemen from Wrentham, Mass. He was a landowner with a wife and two sons. Noah Pratt was one of the guys, well liked, and someone you could count on. He was a common man, a farmer, a builder of homes and furniture, a planemaker, and a church-going man. Noah loved hunting and fishing – and above all he loved the freedom he fought for and passed on to us. Clearly he was one of us – an average sort of guy. I think if he were here with us today, Noah is the kind of guy we might meet out on the open road riding a Harley-Davidson, enjoying the freedom he fought for!

---

25   The Journals of Addison Pratt (son of Henry, grandson of Noah), p4

4   Finding Noah

This story began with the search for a wooden plane to add to my collection in the late 1990s. I had aspired to doing fine woodworking for some 30 years. Through most of this time I'd collected planes and other antique tools for use on my bench – not a real "collection" from a collector's point of view I suppose. As I became more experienced in my work I realized the importance of mouldings and how they affected the esthetics of the furniture and room interiors I made. I came to realize, as Noah certainly understood, that these moulding details make my work come alive – make it something special. Conversely, without the moulding details the finest work is plain and unremarkable - almost Shakeresque. Realizing this I decided to save enough money to buy an old crown moulding plane used to make moulding around the ceiling, fireplace mantle, or cabinet top as in the picture below.

Figure 15: Kitchen framework around stove all in solid cherry including timbers, crotch figured raised panel and hand carved fleur-de-lis, with crown moulding at top - author's work, photo by Bob Poull

As I searched for the right plane, I also became mesmerized by this small group of 18th century planemakers that fought in the Revolution. They were mentioned in tool collectors' books and articles, but only in passing. The real focus was always the tool and the maker – not the history. For me, how the maker lived and worked in this historic time was the main event. I found it incredible that it was possible I might own something made by one of

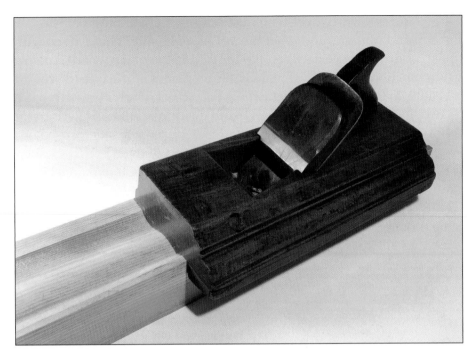

Figure 16: Crown moulding plane by Noah Pratt of cherry c1776 resting on a piece of crown made by this plane. Author's collection, photo by Bob Poull

these patriots from early New England. It seemed unreal – these are not common items and shouldn't I need to be a museum to have the right to own something this special?

Crown moulding planes of any age are quite rare at flea markets, and I eventually found mine at a tool meet in 1999. The N*P mark on the toe was not identified or recorded anywhere. Looking past this and the plane's shabby appearance, I sensed the craftsmanship and color of the wood was beautiful beneath the dirt. Many of my tools were acquired because of the beauty of their materials and details even though they were not generally sought after as 'collectable' by others. I decided an unknown 18th century plane meant more to me then a known planemaker from a later period. At the end of the meet I was able to negotiate a fair price and beamed all the way home with my newfound treasure. Really, I had no clue what I'd just done or the affect this plane would have on my life.

After very careful repairs, I re-oiled the wooden parts of the plane and was quite pleased to see it come back to life – almost as if by magic! The cherry wood is most beautiful and many have commented on the rich color and patina. The unusually fine moulded details on the side of the plane make the large size seem almost delicate, and it certainly is one of the most beautiful tools I've ever seen. For most of five years I was satisfied that I was indeed lucky to have found it. To me, having an identified maker's mark on the plane worth lots of money to collectors could not increase the value I placed on the plane's workmanship and beauty.

As time went by I did not worry over who made this plane, but I did occasionally think about his makeup and training, and what kind of work he might have done with the plane. The most basic difference between the 18th and 19th century wooden planes is their "look". This is a function of the additional details on planes of the late 18th century that add to their beauty, making some of them almost an object of art. I learned that 18th century planes made here in the colonies were often made by individual housewrights and joiners for use in their own work. If the craftsman who made this plane was focused on making fine furniture or fine household trim, then he was trained with an eye for beauty and accustomed to taking the time to add fine details to his work. Craftsman of this makeup would be almost compulsive about adding fine details to everything they made – even their tools. By 1800 this was lost as specialists made their entire living making planes. They had neither the training nor the eye, the time nor inclination to make their tools ornate. By 1800 they were after all, just tools.

Figure 17: Solid black walnut mantle 4" thick with crown moulding, author's work, photo by Bob Poull

So I came to realize that N*P was not just the mark of the person that made this fine tool, but likely the person who made it for his own use. It also dawned on me there were no other user's marks anywhere on the plane as are commonly found. Perhaps N*P was the only one who ever used the plane? It also occurred to me he may have been a housewright, for the crown moulding the plane made was big enough to be used in the parlor or main room and too big for most furniture. Still, the block of cherry wood the plane is made of was over two inches thick and was carefully dried years before the plane was made - there is not a single check or crack in it. If there was dried cherry in the shop, this craftsman was also building furniture.

Now the idea came over me to find this person who perhaps built homes and furniture like I do, and it really took ahold of me. Now I began to dream that it might even be possible to find a home or piece of furniture over 200 years old that this plane was used to make. While this would be even more impossible then looking for a needle in a haystack, collectors have found two moulding planes made by J. Hemings that he used in making window sash mouldings during a restoration of Monticello under the direction of Thomas Jefferson in the 1790's.[26] Now the dream having totally consumed me, I finally decided to dig a little and try to find out who N*P might have been.

I began by going through the entire "P" section of *American Wooden Planes*[27], looking for someone that could have been N*P c1750-1800 in the general New England area. There were only four potential makers mentioned within these criteria. The one that caught my eye was Henry Pratt of Wrentham, Mass. Henry was born in 1771, too late to have made the cherry crown. However, the maker could have been his father - and it was interesting to note that there is an example of a "cherry complex molding plane" made by Henry c 1800. Also, according to *American Wooden Planes,* another planemaker Nathan Pratt was thought to be a descendant of Henry. It was common to name children after their father or grandfather and to carry on the family trade – so I thought it possible that Henry's father was also a Nathan and could be N*P in the mid 1700s timeframe. This possibility and the fact that Henry Pratt made at least one cherry plane led me to search further and the eventual discovery that his father was Noah Pratt (not Nathan as I thought). I also learned that Nathan was Henry's brother – so here we had the potential that Noah had taught both his sons how to make planes. At this point Noah Pratt became the primary focus of my search.

Simply finding Noah Pratt was the easiest part of my search because Wrentham records show Noah and Hannah as Henry's parents. Wrentham records also show Noah and Hannah's marriage, the births of their children, and Noah's service in the Minuteman Company. However, following the 1790 Census they seemed to drop off the end of the earth – gone and no clue where. So I lost sight of Noah for a while, and I realized that really "finding" or knowing anything more about him beyond a few vital statistics would be more difficult. There was still no clue that Noah worked in wood, much less made planes. Time passed and I got a lucky break when a local librarian's search found Capt Noah Pratt buried in Winchester, NH. This led me to the home and woodshop in Winchester, and the rest of their story covered in a later chapter. Pardon me if you feel I've droned on about this, but I've just condensed years of searching into the single paragraph that you just read.

---

26 *The Gristmill* June 2006, p17 newsletter of the Mid-West Tool Collectors Association
27 A guide to the Makers of American Wooden Planes by Emil & Martyl Pollak, 4th Edition Revised by Thomas L. Elliott

Figure 18: Multiple planes used to create a crown moulding as done in England, planes in author's collection, photo by Bob Poull

The crown moulding plane was a uniquely American invention almost never seen in England, where they used a number of smaller planes successively next to each other to complete such a wide moulding. Americans used a single wide plane as a labor saving device and the resulting mouldings would be more uniform. On the flip side, our crown moulding planes required more power to work and often needed a second helper to pull the plane as the master pushed it through the wood. This was made somewhat easier by the abundance of old growth white pine which cut almost like butter, but it was still a lot of work.

We know that Noah was serious about making this plane by just looking at it, but there are more subtle clues to how seriously Noah pursued his work. Remember the block of cherry wood the plane is made of was carefully dried a long time before the plane was made. Noah also was serious enough to have a stamp made with his initials N*P to mark the planes that he made. The N*P is most definitely a "makers mark" stamp and not the more common ones made by users to mark their tools. Perhaps this was just pride in his work, or maybe he thought early in his career that he might make more planes for sale like his neighbor, Cesar Chelor, mentioned earlier. Beyond all this, we know that planes were most important to Noah because they were the lifeblood of his work.

Figure 19: Makers mark N*P on the front of crown moulding plane, photo by Bob Poull

To give an idea of how much a housewright's existence in the 1700s depended on the common plane, let's consider the mass of work necessary to raise just a single home. A study focused on the eighteenth century housewright[28] used the Lowell-Whittier House built in 1787 in Metheun, Massachusetts to determine how much wood went into it and the variety of planes used. While the home had just 1,750 square feet of living space, it was determined there were 7,500 board feet of white pine surfaced one side only for flooring, wall panels, and siding. Another 2,000 board feet of pine was surfaced all four sides and additional joinery was done to make doors, window frames, paneled room ends and trim mouldings for this modest home.

---

28 Eighteenth-Century Woodworking Tools, Papers Presented May 19-22, 1994, Edited by James M. Gaynor, p139, from the paper The Joiner's Trade and the Wooden Plane in 18th Century New England, Ted Ingraham

So you can understand the magnitude of work, this pile of white pine boards was 10 feet long, 10 feet wide and 10 feet tall. Anyway you look at it that's a lot of tens. The work required to surface-plane and mould all this lumber into a single house is almost beyond comprehension – months of effort. The work required a minimum of 22 planes and would have been nigh onto impossible without them. For Noah to build a home without these planes would be like many of us trying to work without a computer, email or cellphone. This set of planes was as essential to Noah Pratt in his work as the right bat was to Babe Ruth or Hank Aaron. Keep in mind these were just the boards to finish the home and make it livable, and don't include the pile of timbers joined to make the house structure itself.

By the 1770s all of the boards and timbers needed for a new home would have been cut at the local water-powered sawmill, which were found all over New England. This means Noah didn't have to pit-saw each timber, but building a home was still a huge effort. As recently as our servicemen returning from WWII, families got together and built homes for themselves as long as one of them had enough background to get this done. Today I don't think this is very common, but I can tell you that, having done it myself, building your own home like Noah did brings a lot of emotions that others never experience. Today people think it is quite an effort just to watch a general contractor build their home, and many marriages have been broken by the stress. I can tell you that literally building it yourself, with the help of a few friends and family, is a humbling experience.

Building my own timberframed home and studio at age 37 in the "prime of my life", I finally came hard up against the realization that I might not be able to do something just because I put my mind to it. My wife Dee and I were living in a small trailer on site with nothing more than a generator for electricity the first few months. We worked through the hottest drought that summer, the coldest October on record, and a rare 12 inches of thunder snow in mid December. At that point I realized how much my work had been slowed. With the dead of winter coming on,

Figure 20: Snow inside the unfinished home - winter of 1987 upon us.

the walls of the main house were up, but not the rafters and roof. I realized I was in a pretty tenuous situation. If I couldn't get the roof on and closed in, the project would stall and might be seriously threatened over winter. I was blessed with a few family members and a close friend that came out on weekends to help us. With the help of one of the few contractors I hired, we rushed the rafters into place and then threw up roof sheeting working long hours into the dead of night with temps dropping below zero. The last of the roof shingles went on in mid January so I could continue my work inside through the winter cold. Today, it is hard for me to think about that time and not reflect on all the hardships that Noah and the rest of our colonists overcame with the help of their family and neighbors.

I don't know about Noah and others that have built their own homes over the centuries, but for me there are deep rooted feelings that have not faded even after 20 years. Of course there is great pride in looking at what was accomplished, the quality and beauty that was created in this home. There is great pride in how the fireplace alone keeps my family warm through the night at 22 degrees below zero. Still, when a really serious storm comes through, my mind harkens back to that late December when things were not so sure – nothing in life was certain. Did I build it well enough – will it stand yet one more test? We have a set of walk-in bay windows just off the living room and when I stand there it's like being right outside with the storm swirling around me, the wind howling in my face driving the snow and this eerie sound like Mick Jagger screaming "Gimme Shelter" at maximum volume:

> *Oh, a storm is threatening*
> *my very life today*
> *If I don't get some shelter*
> *oh yeah, I'm gonna fade away* [29]

Noah never knew Mick Jagger or stereo, but he knew about this most basic need for shelter – and how fragile life and home are in the face of nature.

It has occurred to me that in finding this plane – in finding Noah Pratt – I also found myself. Oh, I don't mean I was lost or didn't know who I was or that I needed some psychobabble to set my life straight. I mean I have often felt that I should have lived 200 years ago. This is not just because my work would have been more appreciated back then, but even more so because the rule that I measure life by was the accepted standard in society at that time. I try to live my life being honest, caring about my work and those around me, focused on what's important in life. I don't take the easy way out even if that is more popular, and when I give my word you can go to the bank on it. I believe we should try to lift those around us rather than step over them to get ahead. Looking at society today you can see this measure is as antiquated as Noah's crown moulding plane – quaint perhaps, but useless. Finding Noah was sort of like glancing in a mirror and catching a fleeting glimpse of him as a reflection of what I might have been, rather than seeing myself stranded here out of place and time. This feeling of déjà vu only intensified as I discovered Noah's work as a housewright, timberframer, furniture maker, and mentor – all work that I have taken to heart and do to the best of my ability.

---

29 Gimme Shelter by Mick Jagger and Keith Richards, Let it Bleed album 1969

"Shelter from the Storm"
Photographs by Melissa D. Hanley

5   Why Massachusetts

As I learned more about the American Revolution and the role that Noah Pratt played, eventually I came to realize that the early incendiary events and the actual flashpoint of the war itself all happened in and around Boston, Massachusetts. A short list of these events includes the Boston Massacre, Boston Tea Party, such intense resistance to the Stamp Act that the King quartered troops right in Boston, closing the port of Boston, the Battles of Lexington and Concord – and of Bunker Hill, and finally the colonials forcing the British out of Boston in 1776.

Even after considering this, few of us immediately appreciate that the events in Massachusetts all happened prior to the Declaration of Independence. To be sure, the other colonies were deeply involved in discussing these events – and many of them sent letters of support to Massachusetts (don't worry – we're right behind you). The Vermont Green Mountain Boys captured the big guns at Fort Ticonderoga that ultimately forced the British out of Boston, and some of the colonies sent troops, powder, and money to help mount the siege of Boston. Virginia provided our first commander in chief, but George Washington didn't take command of the troops around Boston till after the Battle of Bunker Hill. Really, it was the men and women of Massachusetts that actually brought the 'push and shove' with England to a boiling point over the course of ten years, put themselves on the line, took the first casualties, and fired the 'shot heard round the world'. "Massachusetts was not just the leader of the rebellion, through this period it *was* the rebellion."[30] Why the people of Massachusetts and not one of the other colonies? What was it about Noah Pratt and his neighbors around Boston that drove them to these extraordinary events?

★   ★   ★   ★   ★

In his seven-volume *History of the United States* published in 1882, George Bancroft tells us "The settlement of New England was a result of implacable differences between Protestant dissenters and the established Anglican Church in England."[31] If this were not enough of an understatement, he goes on to muse "Who will venture to measure the consequences of actions by the humility or the remoteness of their origin?" The Protestant dissenters Bancroft refers to were the forefathers of the Pilgrims over 100 years prior to the landing at Plymouth Rock in 1620. Noah Pratt was the direct descendant of the first two groups of dissenters who founded this colony. Although I am not a fan of church history, this is so central to who Noah Pratt and these New England settlers were and how the Revolution began, that we must spend a moment reflecting on it.

---

30 Decisive Day – The Battle for Bunker Hill by Richard M. Ketchum, p58
31 History of the United States, George Bancroft 1882 Vol 1, p177

As the 1500s began, the Roman Catholic Church held domain over most of Europe and England. However, there was a great protest led by Luther, Calvin, and others who felt the Church had gone astray. This spiritual and intellectual movement held that the Catholic Church had been caught up in needless ritualism, fancy churches, vestments, and a growing hierarchy of bishops and administrators going up to the Pope in Rome – all dictating laws on how to run peoples' spiritual lives. Some of these dissenters called for a Reformation of the Roman Catholic Church to discard these trappings and re-focus simply on the word of God found in the Bible. They posed that each person is responsible for his or her own salvation, is capable of spiritual thought as profound as any priest, and that a congregation of simple folks should have the freedom to decide their own spiritual matters without the need for bishops or the Pope.

Ironically this is the same set of circumstances that surrounded the coming of Christ. His message to the Hebrews was that they had taken ten simple commandments – and turned them into a whole religious hierarchy of priesthood and books of law dictating what was holy. For example, the simple commandment to "Keep Holy the Lord's Day" was further dictated by man as you can't walk more than xx steps on the Sabbath or you've sinned. In the New Testament Christ said, let's try again – and I'll give you just two rules this time – Love God and Love thy neighbor. Well, after 1,500 years the Catholic Church had taken the two rules and magnified them into a huge organization of priesthood, property, and laws. No wonder there were dissenters!

Throughout Europe, large groups of dissenters split off from the Catholic Church and went their own way spiritually without disrupting their governments. However in England Henry VIII took advantage of this unrest and the Reformation to denounce the Pope and split the entire Church of England away from Rome. This was more a political move then anything spiritual – after all Henry wanted a divorce and the Pope had refused. Way beyond spirituality, I should guess Henry also realized that he could take all the power and the wealth – all the church property for his own and end the stream of money being sent to Rome. To give you an idea of the scope of this, at the time fully one third of all property in England was owned by the Catholic Church!

Not everybody in England welcomed this move. Many wanted to remain Catholic, so Henry left the Church of England looking pretty much like the Catholic Church – except he now took the place of the Pope. However, the dissenters realized there had been no reformation at all, and continued to press for change closer to the "pure" word of God – and **thus they were called Puritans**. The monarchy was not real fond of dissenters or "free thinkers" on religious matters. Really now, if a group of common peasants could decide they no longer needed the Pope, who knows where that might lead?

While the dissention had begun on purely religious grounds, in England it now took on a more urgent priority with direct relation ultimately to our American Revolution. Now that England had tightly bound the church and state into one entity, anyone dissenting against any spiritual matter also found themselves at odds with the King – and could be charged with treason. Challenging any church law as simple as "don't eat meat on Friday", could ultimately be used to imprison, torture, or put someone to death. All the liberty and freedom that English subjects had come to cherish over hundreds of years was suddenly threatened. In our own time, this same danger is seen in some Islamic states where their religious laws are actually the state law – giving us the example of a pregnant woman being sentenced to be stoned to death because it is obvious she had intercourse out of wedlock – even when the pregnancy was the result of a brutal rape!

Things got pretty bloody for the Puritans and a group of them gave up trying to reform England and moved to Leiden outside of Amsterdam to take up residence and practice their faith as they saw fit. Portions of this same group of Puritans eventually traveled to the New World establishing the earliest settlement in New England founding Plymouth Colony in Massachusetts in 1620. We think of these Pilgrims as that dour group in robes and strange hats, and so they were. However, they were Puritans, and commonly called "Pilgrims" simply because they were foreigners who had traveled to far-away and strange lands in search of some holy place.

Right about now you've probably had enough religion and wish I'd get back to motorcycles, horses, horse manure, or almost any other topic. So let's take a pop culture break and lighten up a little. Charles M. Schulz often drew his famous Peanuts characters to remind us of the real importance of people and events in our life. In *A Charlie Brown Thanksgiving* Schulz drew Snoopy and Woodstock as Pilgrims to remind us that they founded our Thanksgiving celebration, and then poked fun at their ridiculous costumes. Imagine Snoopy carrying around a blunderbuss[32] dumbed down as a cork gun.[33] We will see that the Pilgrims not only founded Thanksgiving, they played a significant role in founding our country as well.

In Massachusetts the Pilgrims came to form the Congregational Church – a form perhaps unique to New England. They were basically Protestant, but the individual congregations chose who would lead them, and were only loosely related to congregations in other towns. Bishops and other clergy in the church hierarchy were simply eliminated. Each congregation owned its own property, built their own meeting house, and stopped making donations toward supporting the church hierarchy they'd just "downsized". This simplified form was of course contrary to the Church of England, which lost the property, the donations, and the spiritual control over these people. Ironically, the Pilgrims took from the Church of England just what Henry VIII took from the Roman Catholic Church just 100 years prior.

---

32 A blunderbuss is a short large bore gun flared at the end often associated with the Pilgrims.
33 Sorry, we will all have to use our imagination because Snoopy and Woodstock declined my invitation to have their cartoon picture included here.

While the early Congregational churches broke from the hierarchy of the Church of England, they continued the practice that persons had to be a baptized member of the church to be a voting citizen in their town. In fact, the elders who members voted to run the church also ran the town, the courts, and everything else. However, Old South Church in Boston formed when a group of dissenters broke away from the First Church of Boston. The First Church was Congregational, so really now we have dissenters breaking away from dissenters – where would the chaos end? This new group formed Old South Church because they felt that religious conversion should not be a requirement for citizenship and voting. This was the ultimate statement that people shouldn't be forced to practice a particular religion as had been the case with their forefathers in England, still in recent memory.

At Old South in Boston we now have a congregation that rejected the old form of church hierarchy and literally decided to separate church from state – a huge event in American history. Benjamin Franklin was baptized in Old South. Other notable members include Judge Samuel Sewall who wrote the first pamphlet advocating the abolition of slavery in the colonies. Samuel Adams was also a member, and the Sons of Liberty used the Old South as the springboard for the Boston Tea Party. Paul Revere, also a Puritan, was at the Boston Tea Party and made the famous midnight ride to warn the people of Lexington and Concord that the British were coming. It is most ironic that the warning lanterns (one if by land, two if by sea) were hung that night in the belfry of Old North Church - which was The Church of England. It seems that even they had a dissenter in the form of their deacon who was willing to hang the warning lanterns as a signal for Paul Revere.

Figure 21: Old South Meeting House nearly 300 years on this spot in Boston, courtesy of National Park Service

★ ★ ★ ★ ★

So, here we have some pretty serious dissension founding Massachusetts over 150 years leading up to the Revolution. The Mayflower Compact drafted and signed by that first group of Pilgrims in 1620 defined a new form of government for Massachusetts where the congregations (towns) held meetings and every landowner had an equal say or 'vote' to choose leaders and decide how things would be done. The very seeds of independence were sown in this single document! Years later Thomas Jefferson would call the

Massachusetts town meetings "the wisest invention ever devised by the wit of man for the perfect exercise of self-government".[34] From the earliest settlement, Massachusetts was different – a veritable Petri dish nourishing a new culture of thinking and politics in this new land.

Not everyone who lived in early Massachusetts was a dissenter, but the Puritans settled en-masse around Boston and down toward Providence, RI – Wrentham included. Those willing to practice religion as they were told had mostly stayed back in England or migrated to other colonies. These Puritan settlers were not followers. They had strong beliefs, had challenged their king, were willing to face unthinkable hardship and death – ultimately getting into small ships and traveling to a new and foreign land. They were dissenters, leaders, free thinkers, the very basis of Yankee ingenuity, and they were most certainly "trouble makers" from the British point of view.

The Revolution in Massachusetts was not just the work of a few hotheaded intellectuals stirring up the masses in Boston. Remember the 20,000 Massachusetts men massed outside Boston on less than 24 hours notice? In a similar but much smaller incident two years earlier, British General Gage noted in a letter to London "Thou the people are not held in high estimation by the troops, yet they are numerous, worked up to a fury, and not a Boston rabble *but the freeholders and farmers of the country.*"[35] General Gage realized he was faced with a majority of the common people of the region – not just a few trouble makers in Boston.

The people of Massachusetts declared their independence with their blood a full year before the rest of the colonies signed the Declaration of Independence. Given the makup and history of these people it should come as no surprise that the fight for our freedom began there. Noah Pratt descended from the staunchest Puritan leaders that founded this colony. He was the product of their ideals and thinking. Just look at the brief family tree on the next page to get an idea of Noah Pratt's Puritan lineage. Noah Pratt is the most perfect example of the "freeholders and farmers of the countryside" and why the American Revolution began in Massachusetts.

---

34 The Unknown American Revolution by Gary B. Nash p 18
35 Ibid p 181

Noah Pratt's Puritan Ancestors & Family History
in the Congregational Church

Henry Pratt, born c1570 in England, was a non-conformist minister imprisoned for preaching the gospel contrary to the Church of England. He was one of more than 400 still in prison when his son Phinehas left for the new world.	Degory Priest is one of the group of Pilgrims persecuted in England who moved his family first to Leiden in Holland, and then to Massachusetts arriving with the very first group of Pilgrims on the Mayflower in 1620. Degory Priest was a signer of the Mayflower Compact[36].
Phinehas Pratt[37] was born in England, arrived in Massachusetts with the second group of Pilgrims on the ship Sparrow in 1622, and married ⟶	Mary Priest - daughter of Degory Priest.

Noah's grandfather, Henry Pratt, was chosen a selectman in the town of Needham[38] and was a respected leader of the church.

Noah's father, Oliver Pratt, was baptized in the First Church of Needham[39] on Oct 17th, 1725.

Our planemaker, Noah Pratt[40], married Hannah Sterns of Wrentham and named their firstborn son Henry. In doing so they broke the pervasive practice of naming the firstborn after the father. The name Henry held great significance to this family, not just because of Noah's grandfather, but going all the way back to Phinehas's father, one of the first Puritan preachers in England.

In 1792 Noah and family moved to Winchester NH, and Noah was appointed by the congregation to the committee responsible for building the new meeting house. Prior to building, Noah purchased no less than 6 pews in support of the new church.[41]

Noah's oldest son, Henry, was one of the first organ makers in America, and his first organ was made for the Congregational Church in Winchester. One of the pews that Noah had purchased was still in Henry's estate when it was settled at the time of his death.[42]

36 *Phinehas Pratt's Descendents 1622-1987* by Priscilla Lorena Pratt Briggs
37 Phinehas Pratt (b c1570 England d 4-19-1680 Charlestown, MA) per previous ref.
38 Henry Pratt (b 6-5-1685 Hingham, d 11-1-1750 in Needham) per *Clark's History of Needham*, by Clark
39 Oliver Pratt (b 1710 in Needham, d 5-17-1763 in Newton) per Mormons
40 Noah Pratt (b3-15-1748 Wrentham or Newton? d 1-4-1807 Winchester, NH m Hannah Sterns 5-3-1770
41 The History of Cheshire County NH, section on Winchester NH, p569-570
42 New Hampshire Cheshire County Probate, Henry Pratt Inventory Sept 21, 1841

6 The Turning Point

Following the Battle of Lexington and Concord, the Americans settled in to keeping the 5,000 British regulars bottled up in Boston. While the Americans numbered some 20,000 at the start, many units like Noah Pratt's returned home after a couple of weeks sitting around waiting for something to happen. These men had not brought the clothing or food for an extended stay – and there were important crops to plant or the colony would starve come winter.

As news of the Battle at Lexington and Concord spread through the colonies, additional units came from New Hampshire, Connecticut, and Rhode Island. These units came of their own accord and were certainly most welcome because the Continental Army had not yet been formed. Even so, the American force shrunk to something less than 10,000 men – still twice the British garrison they watched. These were mostly Massachusetts militia with a northern command and forces centered in Cambridge, and another covering the southern approaches based in the town of Roxbury. These commanders were Massachusetts militia, and not literally in command of men from the other colonies – except by gentlemen's agreement. It was immediately apparent this was a mass of men with no one to organize and lead it as a single disciplined unit. Firearms, powder, and supplies of all kinds were urgently needed.

During this time Britain tired of General Gage's inability to get things under control, and they dispatched three of their most experienced generals along with reinforcements to Boston. They left England unaware of the Battle of Lexington & Concord and its results. Upon hearing the disturbing news from a passing ship near Boston, General John Burgoyne shouted "What – ten thousand peasants keep five thousand of the King's troops shut up? Well, let *us* get in and we'll soon find elbowroom!"[43] The three generals, considered the best that England had to offer, landed in Boston on May 25th and reported to General Gage.

Amidst the colonial disorganization, the Battle of Bunker Hill happened just 60 days after Lexington & Concord – and just 3 weeks after the arrival of the new British generals. The British were well aware that their position would be defenseless if the colonists fortified Bunker Hill across the Charles River to the north just above the city of Charlestown. Recall that the British had occupied this high ground the night following the Battle of Lexington & Concord. However, they abandoned the hill and Charlestown as they retreated back to Boston the next day. General Gage had made it known that he would burn Charlestown if the rebels tried to occupy Bunker Hill – and for a time neither side made a move. However, the newly arrived British reinforcements sitting all pent-up in Boston must have felt tremendous pressure to do something – anything but sit there. On June 15, 1775 the Colonial Committee of Safety, concerned about the British reinforcements and information

---

43 *Decisive Day – The Battle for Bunker Hill* by Richard M. Ketchum, p2

that they intended to make a move, finally ordered the fortification of Bunker Hill to prevent it from being taken. The next day Colonel William Prescott was ordered to fortify Bunker Hill.

Everyone knew the colonist's fortification would draw an immediate attack from the British. Through the haze of history and time and from the vantage point of a Monday-morning quarterback, the American commander seems more concerned with the vulnerability of the main army around his Cambridge headquarters. He appears unwilling to commit enough men, proper equipment, arrangements for a relief force, or even the most basic supplies of food and water to the men assigned to Bunker Hill. That evening, under conditions that should have foretold certain failure, Col Prescott and his force set out for Bunker Hill. No one could have foreseen the miracle they were about to deliver for the cause of freedom.

★   ★   ★   ★   ★

Col Prescott was a wise choice to take command and challenge the British that day. He had experience in the French wars and the respect of the regiment who voted him as their Colonel.[44] The men formed up at about 6:00 the evening of June 16th having been ordered to parade with blankets, provisions for a day, and "all the intrenching tools in this encampment".[45] They left Cambridge Common with Col Prescott leading the column. The 800 Massachusetts men were met on the road by 200 men of Connecticut under General Israel Putnam – "Old Put" as he was generally known.

Having reached Charlestown area, somehow a decision was made to fortify Breed's Hill, which was a lower elevation and within range of cannon fire from the British fleet and batteries on Beacon Hill in Boston. No one knows why they chose this over the superior position that Bunker Hill would have provided. The decision made, their engineer marked out the fort, and the men began digging the earthworks even as they heard the clocks of Boston striking the hour of midnight.[46]

How could anyone expect an inexperienced engineer to lay out a fort in the dark, and volunteer soldiers to erect such a fort in the middle of the night with less than 5 hours till daybreak and certain discovery? Well, these volunteer soldiers were almost all farmers – and they were experts in the use of a pick and shovel. The men worked quietly, confidently, and with great speed. They had no sleep, little food, and ran out of water before daybreak. At 4:00 am the lookout aboard one of the British warships spotted the work, and the ship came around and fired their guns at them – waking the entire British garrison in Boston.

---

44 *Decisive Day – The Battle for Bunker Hill* by Richard M. Ketchum, p98
45 Ibid p91
46 Ibid p111

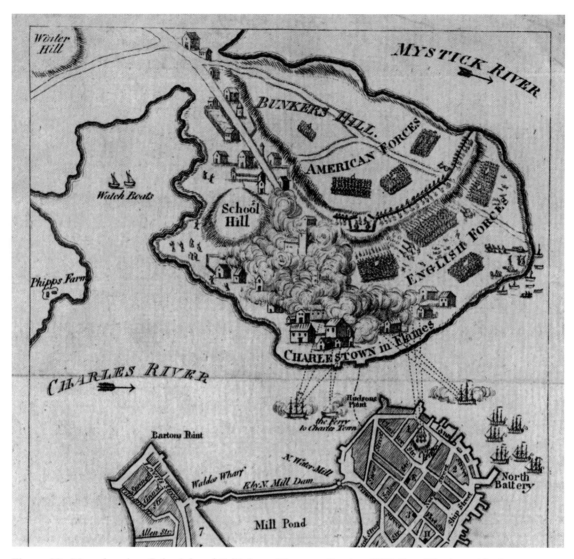

Figure 22: Map showing Colonial and British positions on Bunker Hill, tip of Boston at bottom. T Robson 1778 courtesy of Library of Congress, Geography and Map Division

In the dawning light Prescott realized that his left flank down to the Mystic River was unprotected, and the British could take their fort with no effort at all (as seen in the map above). He put the men to work to correct this best they could. Most of these volunteers had never been to war, and the sound of the big guns was fearful even before the first casualty was taken. But Col Prescott was everywhere strengthening and encouraging the men – and their work continued. Apparently about this time, General Gage was viewing the rebel fort from Boston, handed his telescope to a Tory citizen who was standing at his side, and asked if he knew the tall commanding figure standing on the wall. The man responded that was William Prescott – his own brother-in law. When Gage asked if he would fight, the man replied "I cannot answer for his men, but Prescott will fight you to the gates of hell".[47]

---

47 *Decisive Day – The Battle for Bunker Hill* by Richard M. Ketchum, p127

The British decided to make short work of it and throw the entire elite corps of every regiment in Boston at the rebels in a full frontal assault. The British army believed almost to a man that the rebels would not stand and fight. Though they moved without delay, the standard course of preparation for the troops to embark lost many hours, allowing the rebels to complete their work on the fort. All the while the British big guns continued to fire.

By now the American force was exhausted, faced with a fierce battle, and feeling abandoned. Twice they had sent for reinforcements to no avail. Finally two additional regiments were ordered to march – but this was about noon as the redcoats were marching to the foot of the wharf to embark for Charlestown. Time was running out.

★   ★   ★   ★   ★

The British boats had rowed some 1,500 redcoats to Morton's Point outside Charlestown in the first two waves. General Howe - realizing the fortification was now more complete with additional rebel works blocking his flanking movement – called for yet more reinforcements. While waiting, the British regulars took their packs off and ate lunch in full sight – but out of gunshot of the rebels. Meanwhile the two new regiments arrived and further strengthened the American flank alongside the main fort down to the Mystic River. Their defenses were little more then split rail fences stuffed with tall grass with a ditch to help hide the men, and a stone wall stacked on the beach.

About this time Gen Howe ordered the town of Charlestown torched so he would not be threatened by rebel snipers from that vantage point. In very little time the 500 structures that made up the town were in flames. Howe's reinforcements had landed, and he formed the attack in two sections. One attack was on the center and left aimed directly at the earthwork fort – and Howe himself led the attack on the side where the fence and stone wall stood down to the Mystic River.

Figure 23: Charlestown in flames as the British attack Bunker Hill. Engraving by Lodge from drawing by Miller. Courtesy of the National Archives and Records Administration

The British attack stepped off about 2:30 in the afternoon. The Americans had already marched and dug for 21 hours with no sleep and little food. The majority of the men were untested volunteers numbering at peak about 1,500. They clearly saw this superior force, that eventually grew to 2,500 well trained and equipped British soldiers, marching in attack formation with bayonets glimmering in the sun. Every man knew they had precious little gunpowder – they were ordered to "wait till you see the white's of their eyes" to make every shot count. All the while the cannon pounded and Charlestown burned – were they not at the gates of hell itself? The waiting must have been horrible, seeing this overwhelming force – the finest infantry in the world coming up at them – about to wash over them. Would the rebels break at this show of force as the British were certain they would?

The redcoats were as close as 50 feet to the stone wall on the beach when the order came to fire. The American walls erupted in smoke, pouring a withering fire on the redcoats marching at them. The British devastation was horrible – whole ranks lying dead. Incredibly, the British attack stumbled and then turned into a shattered retreat – some of the men actually running all the way back to the boats. Down at the stonewall the Americans could see the British dead "as thick as sheep in a fold" lying at their feet.[48]

Within 15 minutes Howe reformed a second attack now focused on the rail fence and directed the other thrust to take the fort without waiting for him. The second attack was just as disastrous. One British officer reported that many of their finest companies lost 75-90% dead and wounded along the rail fence – some companies had only 5 men left standing. The results were just as devastating for the attack on the fort. The British lines actually ran into the men in front of them as they were being mowed down by the American fire. Once again, the British ranks turned and ran.[49]

Howe decided he had no choice but to mount a third direct charge. He called for yet more reinforcements and focused the attack directly against the fort. This time he presented his troops in columns till the last minute to present less of a target – and the men marched more quickly not weighed down by their full pack and gear. Unknown to the British, Prescott's men were almost entirely out of powder. They broke open what was left from their small canon – but they knew full well there was not enough powder for a third attack. The Americans presented the same withering fire at close range – with the same devastating effect – but only for a while till the powder ran out. At the fort wall, Major John Pitcairn, who had led the British charge on Lexington Common just two months earlier, called to his marines that the enemy had abandoned the fort – when they heard a boy inside call "We're not all gone". By all reports, at that moment a black soldier in the fort named Salem Prince shot Pitcairn through the head.[50] Salem Prince is thus memorialized in Jonathan Trumbull's famous painting of the battle.

48 *Decisive Day – The Battle for Bunker Hill* by Richard M. Ketchum, p158
49 Ibid p162
50 Ibid p174.

Figure 24: Battle of Bunkers Hill by Jonathan Trumbull (oil on canvas) in 1786 can be seen at the Museum of Fine Arts in Boston Mass

Even now, there was a moment where the British line wavered for the third time. Prescott later reported that just one more round of fire could have carried the day – but the powder was gone. The redcoats began pouring around the end of the fort and over the walls – bayonets at the ready. Inside everything was dust and smoke and confusion. The British struck with anger using their bayonets. The Americans fought with musket stocks, stones, and fists. Prescott realized there was no chance and ordered the retreat. The Americans suffered their worst losses now, but were saved from total destruction by a valiant rear-guard action presented by the last two regiments who had joined as the battle began. These units at the rail fence were not involved in the third attack and had the powder left to save the rest of the force as it retreated.[51]

Tragically, in the last moments of the battle Joseph Warren was killed, shown as the central figure in Trumbull's painting above. Dr Joseph Warren was president of the Massachusetts Provincial Congress and a prominent member of the Committee of Safety, in which he had voted to fortify Bunker Hill two days earlier. He followed his decision and joined the men in the breastworks that afternoon as the fighting ensued. He had just two days earlier been appointed the second Brigadier General in the Continental Army, and as he entered the fort Col Prescott offered him the command. However, Warren declined to assume authority and instead took for himself a position in the front rank with the rest of the volunteers.[52]

---

51 *History of the United States* by Bancroft V4, p228
52 *History of the United States* by Bancroft V4, p230

He was shot through the head, being one of the last to leave his post on the fort wall. As with so many of our soldiers over 230 years, he paid for our freedom with his life. Joseph Warren left us more than freedom, and we'll talk about this a bit more in the next chapter.

★ ★ ★ ★ ★

The battle itself consumed just 90 minutes – an hour and a half of horror as all battles are. In 1775 whoever held the ground at the end of the day was the victor – and thus the British won. However, General Henry Clinton summed it up best saying "a dear bought victory, another such would have ruined us".[53] The British losses were beyond comprehension. The number of British killed and wounded by General Gage's own report was 1,054 – nearly 50% of his force that carried the burden of attack that day.[54] Some companies were totally decimated. Seventy commissioned officers were wounded and thirteen dead. The fact that General Howe survived was remarkable considering that all 12 of his staff officers were dead or wounded. This single battle accounted for a quarter of all British officer casualties for the entire American Revolution.[55] The oldest soldier could not remember a battle with such serious losses.[56] Only the most contested battles in history like Waterloo and Gettysburg involve such a high percentage of dead and wounded as suffered by the British at Bunker Hill.[57] As a result of Bunker Hill, General Howe never again risked a full-scale frontal assault against entrenched American troops.[58]

Remembering their earlier comment so often re-told in Boston, one British officer wrote "We have got a little elbowroom, but I think we have paid too dearly for it."[59]

In addition to Dr Warren's death, the Americans lost 450 dead and wounded of the 1,500 men that fought, and they felt the sting of defeat. Outside of the men that actually fought the battle, there were examples of insubordination, cowardice, bad planning, and a horrible lack of central leadership. It was years before Americans looked on Bunker Hill as the victory it was – the miracle it was. Amidst all their shortcomings, these 1,500 Americans pitched a direct threat to England, showed their ability to fight with ferocity, and dealt a stunning blow never before seen by the British army. The turning point had been reached; there would be no going back. To his friends Ben Franklin summed it up writing "Americans will fight; England has lost their colonies forever".[60]

---

53   US Forrest Service narrative at the Bunker Hill National Park
54   *Decisive Day – The Battle for Bunker Hill* by Richard M. Ketchum, p 190
55   *Boston 1775 – The Shot Heard Around the World* by Brendan Morrissey, p 66
56   *History of the United States* by Bancroft V4, p 229
57   *The Story of the Revolution*, Henry Cabot Lodge, p 92
58   *Decisive Day – The Battle for Bunker Hill* by Richard M. Ketchum, introduction p xv
59   Ibid p 210
60   *History of the United States* by Bancroft V4, p 231

7   A Brief Interlude

As I write this chapter it is winter here in Wisconsin. This means 5-6 months of frigid cold, ice and snow, trucks throwing salt and sand on the roads – all the bitter enemy of a biker. Last winter for the first time I had the chance to ride three different occasions in places much warmer than home. Accompanying my wife on a business trip to Hawaii, I got to ride on Oahu thanks to the Harley-Davidson Fly 'n Ride program. The ride along the ocean from Waikiki Beach around the south and eastern edge of the island is just a dream – especially for a northern boy in February. A month later I rented a Harley while on business in California and did the PCH (Pacific Coast Highway generally runs alongside the ocean) from Marina Del Rey through Santa Monica, Malibu Beach, and almost up to Santa Barbara – and then returned inland through the Santa Monica Mountains and canyons complete with a stop at the Rock Store. These roads are the stuff of legend including celebrity bikers like Elvis Presley and Jay Leno. Three days later a friend lent me a cycle and led me through the canyons and hills southeast of Los Angeles. The hillsides that formed this road

wound and curved for most of six hours were in full bloom and the air was perfumed, almost intoxicating, sublime. Roger had ridden this often – but he admitted he'd never experienced it quite like that day. Roger retired from Kawasaki Motor Corp the next day, and I heard him explain to his wife "I had to have one last ride". I prayed it wasn't so.

But that was last year; there will be no riding this winter as I am left only with the memory of the warm sun and the wind in my hair riding along the ocean. If I am lucky enough to break the cycle out by mid April, that is still three months away and seems like forever. Even then, in mid April it will be cold riding here – high of 50 degrees in the noon hour if I am lucky. Sunshine is a most welcome riding partner at that temperature. You really learn the meaning of "wind chill" riding a motorcycle in colder weather. I remember the last hour riding home late one spring afternoon a long time ago when the temperature plunged 30 degrees unexpectedly. I was so cold I almost couldn't get my right foot to press the brake pedal. My wife threw me in a tub of hot water to bring my body temperature back up. I'm not complaining – it was my free choice to live in Wisconsin and to ride that day just as any other.

You may think this was just another example that bikers are an irresponsible lot. Not so, I protest. Today I track the weather on a number of different sites and the local news, and I'm amazed at how persistently wrong their predictions are. Even with four different kinds of radar and computer modeling. Once in a while they totally miss their bet and put us in dangerous situations with no warning at all. I often wish I could get a job where I was so persistently wrong and still be a popular celeb in my community.

There is this menacing component of freedom while riding a motorcycle – the freedom to ride in spite of the danger of severe weather, road hazards, and inattentive car drivers we encounter with cell phones at their ear. Our freedom involves an ever lurking danger lying out there unseen, waiting to pounce like a predator on any who let their guard down for a moment while enjoying the thrill of the ride!

There are no seatbelts or airbags riding a motorcycle. After an initial rash of laws mandating use of a helmet, most states have now backed off this kind of over-protectionism and allow us to ride without one. After all, we don't pass laws that scuba divers off the coast of Florida must be housed in the safety of a steel cage in case there are sharks nearby. This kind of protectionism would ultimately force all swimmers on Florida beaches to be in cages too – because you know there might be sharks nearby. It seems lately we hear a lot about shark attacks off Florida beaches – probably something more to do with global warming. My family and I spend time on Virginia Beach many summers, and within the last few years even they had a shark attack a swimmer quite near where we bob in the waves. Wow – you mean there *really might be sharks*? A friend in Florida once confided, "You don't think about that". His point was, if you want the enjoyment of playing in the ocean you have to get past the danger. The danger is real enough so we can't be complacent – but you can't let it consume you or you will never do anything in life. This really is so Jack London. Riding a motorcycle is like that – freedom is like that too.

If we outlaw everything that is dangerous in life there would be no motorcycling, no swimming in the ocean, no skydiving, no mountain climbing, no NASCAR racing, and our kids wouldn't play high school football because occasionally one of them dies. In simple terms, I have the right to ride my Harley 60 mph down a country road dodging potholes, semi trailers coming right at me in the opposite lane just 3 feet away sucking me toward them – with nothing but a bit of leather between me and total destruction. This is the very definition of freedom – for me to choose how to live my life – this lifestyle - in spite of the fact that most folks consider taking this risk just plain stupid. I believe my freedom to ride is what Noah Pratt fought for in the American Revolution. Perhaps you say my thinking is trivial, self-serving, and not worthy of the topic, so come sit with me by the fire and let's mull this over with a glass of warm wine as the snow falls outside.

★ ★ ★ *The Meaning of Freedom* ★ ★ ★

Common men like Noah Pratt didn't leave us a written trail explaining what freedom meant to them or why they fought. However Dr Joseph Warren, who was president of the Massachusetts Provincial Congress and died for our freedom in the last moments on Bunker Hill, believed our government should be:

> *"one which would give every man the greatest liberty to do what he pleases consistent with constraining him from doing injury to another..."* [61]

Joseph Warren believed that our freedom – yours and mine – allows us to do whatever we want as long as my freedom doesn't cause you injury. Injury of course goes beyond physically hurting you to include the legal meaning of injury by taking something from you, like your home or possessions. Today we seem to focus our discussion on freedom of speech or to gather and worship as we please, the basic freedoms defined in the Bill of Rights. But freedom of speech is not the definition of freedom; it is just the first example that comes to mind. The real spirit of freedom that Noah Pratt fought for is letting people alone to enjoy their freedom and not forcing our idea of what that means on them. Joseph Warren died on Bunker Hill with the aspiration that each of us should decide for ourselves what aspect of freedom is important to us and how to enjoy living that freedom every day of our life. When the Declaration of Independence was finally drafted and signed, this is what Thomas Jefferson meant by our unalienable right to life, liberty, and **the pursuit of happiness.**

Again you might say Joseph Warren didn't mean to focus on anything as trivial as my right to ride – but he really did. He said "the greatest liberty to do what I please". To me this is riding. Even though most of you don't ride motorcycles, I hope there are aspects of this in your own life that you can relate to. Can you remember the first time you got the family car? Can you remember the first time you stayed out till 2:00 AM doing whatever you wanted – not just what your family told you to do? Can you remember moving into your first apartment or home? There was this feeling of euphoria and the happiness of deciding things for yourself – do you remember? This was freedom! I hope there is some aspect of freedom like this in your life today – or have you lost it in the rush of daily life lately?

If we agree with Joseph Warren's simple definition of freedom, just think about how 230 years later we have blown this up into libraries of law and hierarchies of government employees making rules telling us what freedom is and how to live it. It sort of reminds me of the situation with the church we discussed earlier. In the process of haggling over the

---

61 *Decisive Day – The Battle For Bunker Hill* by Richard M. Ketchum, p66

laws, it is easy to lose the meaning of religion or freedom. If an ethnic group thinks eating dog meat is a delicacy, we shouldn't throw them in jail for doing so unless it was our dog. It doesn't matter if the majority of us are dog lovers and don't agree with their choice of cuisine. The fact we can and do pass laws like this is a perfect example of freedom denied by our own democracy – by "we the people". This is democracy run amuck! It is imperative that we must not decide that someone's pursuit of happiness is trivial, unnecessary, or wrong just because we don't agree with it. For each of us, our own freedom depends on not telling others how to live theirs. Freedom requires that we maintain a respectful balance amongst each other or it starts to fall apart.

While vacationing on Virginia Beach enjoying the peace of the ocean, one of the most exciting aspects are the military jets that fly over the beach from Langley AFB and Oceana Naval Air Station. Hearing the roar of the jets passing overhead, we always pause to look up – and every time I get goose bumps. Virginia Beach is on the edge of Hampton Roads with a large military presence of the Army, Navy and shipbuilding that dates back to the very beginning of our country. The final decisive battle of the Revolution was fought right there at Jamestown. It's interesting to note that there are Virginia Beach residents who want the noise of the military jets silenced. I understand they feel the noise is a growing nuisance. They forget that the air base was there first and they should not have bought or built these homes close by if they felt they would be injured by the noise. Still, if they could muster enough votes I am certain they would pass a law shutting the base down so they could sit on their deck quietly sipping martinis – enjoying *their freedom* – while refusing to acknowledge the roar of those jets is literally the sound of *our freedom*.

A major US city recently passed a noise ordinance that any biker will be ticketed if their motorcycle can be heard across the street. This is a pretty tough measure against noise, and the law specifically singles out bikers. Cars or trucks, and even lawnmowers that might have the same problem, are not stopped by local law enforcement and challenged with the same sound test. In all fairness, we know that some bikers prefer loud pipes and are not always as considerate of the general population as they could be. Bikers feel this is part of their freedom and they don't actually cause injury to anyone – really just a nuisance. There are many nights I sit in the garden at home and listen to people's dogs from all over the countryside barking up a storm. Often I can hear someone's party clear across the lake – yet these are seldom approached by the police. Still, the folks of this city were able to gather enough votes and passed the law; but that doesn't make it right. If we understand the definition of freedom that Dr Joseph Warren died for, and if we truly believe in our personal choice to decide how to live our freedom in happiness, then we must not pass laws telling others how to live their life as long as they are not causing real injury. We must all be tolerant of each other and how we choose to live our freedom. The next time you hear a group of bikers rumbling by, look closely and you will see the likes of Noah Pratt,

Robert Warren, and the other common men and women of our nation riding by with a grin on their face. I submit that the sound of those motorcycles rumbling by is also the sound of freedom.

One last thought on the dangers of living a free life. I remember screaming down I-80 through Nebraska near dusk one evening a long time ago. I didn't ride with a windscreen that early in life – and a June bug hit me square in the upper lip. I could have passed out - I could have been dead. If you want to enjoy the freedom of riding – you must come to grips with the fact that your freedom is worth dying for. The average citizen cannot bring themselves to this conclusion. They don't understand this lust for freedom in life – and they certainly don't see it as worth dying for. All freedom, however you live it, is worth dying for. Perhaps that is why so many of our servicemen and women and veterans ride motorcycles, because facing this realization changes how you live every day of your life.

8 British out of Boston

Prior to Bunker Hill the need for a central command was not obvious and certainly not a point of common agreement. The units were assembled to protect their homes, land, and liberties from an aggressor British Army. Petitions had gone to the King to get this all straightened out. Defensive positions could be manned by individual units with their own command. Bunker Hill changed that. Now common men began talking not just about preserving their freedom – but also about independence - and the need for a combined army under a single commander became obvious.

On July 3, 1775 General George Washington arrived in Cambridge, Massachusetts to take command of the entire force gathered around Boston. He could see the need for a central staff of officers, uniforms showing rank, more discipline, tents, weapons, and most of all gunpowder. Washington realized the elected officers were often too worried about staying popular to instill proper discipline in the men, and this would need to change. About the only thing they had was food and plenty of alcohol - a staple of any army or navy in those days.

Even as Washington focused on solving his army's problems, he'd brought some baggage of his own with which he would need to deal. As an educated gentleman, he had complete disdain for the common men of New England who dominated this army, as being undisciplined and dirty to the point of being unbearable. While this was a serious problem, Washington needed a bit of attitude adjustment on this point. Most of the men had volunteered and arrived with little more than the clothes on their back. They dug earthworks all day and slept in the open air at night for lack of tents or any other arrangements for their comfort. Men of the era didn't see washing clothes as man's work and we can be quite certain that Washington wasn't washing his own clothes either – so judging the men of New England harshly on this point seems a bit unfair.

In addition, as a southern gentleman and plantation owner, Washington knew well that slave owners back home in Virginia were terrified by the idea of arming and training blacks to fight for their freedom. This was not a concern in Massachusetts where slaves were a very small part of the population, and there were both freemen and slaves fighting alongside whites in the militia units surrounding Boston now under Washington's command. Black men had already served valiantly at Lexington and Bunker Hill. Regardless, Washington gave an early command that blacks, Indians, and young boys would not be allowed in the army – and they were sent home.

Within months Washington would need to reverse this decision as he struggled to maintain enough men to constitute an army. Indeed, with all the other issues nagging at the edges, the most serious problem Washington had to deal with was his disappearing army. Washington faced a problem perhaps unique to the annals of warfare. The army was called up after Lexington & Concord and formed by volunteers in the months of May and June. Most everyone thought there would be a quick appeal to the crown and things would go back to normal. As a result, the volunteer terms were just six months and most of the army was due to evaporate in December as winter set in. So what was worse, running out of gunpowder or running out of army? With Boston surrounded by water, neither the British nor the Americans could mount a large thrust without the risk of high casualties, so the siege of Boston ground on with the volunteer clock ticking away the days.

As autumn came into its own, Col Henry Knox suggested to Washington that the big guns captured at Fort Ticonderoga by Ethan Allen and the Green Mountain Boys be brought down to Boston. Once arrived, they could fortify Dorchester heights across the water from the southern edge of Boston and force the British to withdraw. Many thought moving the guns such a great distance to be impossible, but Henry Knox persuaded Washington. So the cause of American freedom now rested on two separate and distinct miracles – Knox to bring the big guns down to Boston – and Washington to hold the army together long enough to make use of them.

★   ★   ★   ★   ★

Only in America! I wish I could report that Henry Knox was a planemaker, but he was a bookseller from Boston. Imagine a twenty-something junior officer catching the ear of Gen George Washington, but remember the people of Massachusetts were used to speaking their mind on matters of importance. The mission was certainly against all odds, but if it failed at least there wouldn't be thousands of dead volunteers as would be the case with a direct assault on Boston.

Knox set out in mid November – the worst time of year for such an undertaking. He reached Fort Ticonderoga the first week of December and picked which guns to move, a total of 58 mortars and cannon. This was an unbelievable 120,000 pounds of artillery to be transported to Boston. One cannon alone weighed more than 5,000 pounds.[62] To get this done, Henry enlisted local volunteers to help with the transport.

The guns were pulled on sleds by oxen, sometimes in snow and sometimes in mud. On the way south to Albany they crossed the Hudson River four times. On the last crossing one of the largest guns broke through the ice – and was salvaged the next day to continue the trip. Next they had to cross the Berkshire Mountains covered in snow with difficult steep passages both up and down. In all they moved the guns almost three hundred miles through the dead of winter, arriving at Boston near the end of January 1776.

---

62   *1776* by David McCullough, p82

★ ★ ★ ★ ★

Even as this odyssey took place, Washington and his officers somehow managed to re-build the army. Enough of the "old army" stayed on and was augmented by new regiments that came to create the new Continental Army as it now came to be known.[63] Now, with the big guns arrived, Washington called his council of war on Feb 16th to decide their course of action.

The decision was to fortify Dorchester Heights in a single night, just as they did at Bunker Hill – and draw the British out of Boston as they most certainly would respond. However, unlike Bunker Hill, the plans were meticulous covering every detail. Fortifications were fabricated ahead of time to be drug up the hill and set in place quickly. The night of March 4th was chosen, and the men at work hauling the fortifications and guns up to the Heights were in good spirits. Rifle units were designated to cover the work in case the British showed up early. At three in the morning a fresh force of 3,000 men moved in to relieve those who started the work. By first light everything was in place including 20 of the big guns.

The British were once again caught totally by surprise. General Howe was said to have exclaimed "My God, these fellows have done more work in one night than I could make my army do in three months".[64] In simple terms, the 20 colonial guns positioned on the Heights could destroy the British fleet and the entire city of Boston. Even if the British had 2,000 cannon, not a single one could be elevated high enough to hit something on the Heights. Remembering the destruction at Bunker Hill, at least some of the British senior staff officers went on record as saying a direct attack would be folly. The British made a show of moving troops into action, but the weather turned ugly. By 8:00 that same evening the decision was made to abandon Boston.

★ ★ ★ ★ ★

As Washington made his plans for Dorchester Heights, he unwittingly re-introduces Noah Pratt to our story. Realizing his force was still affected by the "downsizing" they had just gone through, Washington called up 2,000 Massachusetts militia to strengthen his force.[65] Noah Pratt of Wrentham was one of those 2,000 men. Recall that Noah marched with his company of Minutemen the previous April and served 11 days as one of the 20,000 men opening the siege of Boston. He returned home and spent the next eight months tending his farm and family. This was just as important as serving in the army, for if the farmers hadn't planted and harvested, the army and the rest of the colony would starve. In those days you couldn't just go down to the Piggly Wiggly or Wal-Mart

---

63 *1776* by David McCullough, p69
64 Ibid p93
65 Ibid p89

Supercenter to restock the pantry. Now in the quiet of winter, Noah Pratt volunteered as one of "Col. L. Robinson's regiment engaged Jan 29 1776; service 2 mos 4 days; regiment raised in Suffolk and York counties; muster roll dated Roxbury."[66]

It would be easy to miss the point that Noah's force of 2,000 men was not Continental Army – they were Massachusetts Militia assigned to Washington's command for a short time. Noah, like many others of his time, continued to serve short stints in the militia through 1780 – but never joined the Continental Army. There was a general distrust of a central standing army through the early history of our country. The colonists had witnessed first-hand the trouble the British Army could cause and many felt more comfortable relying on their own local militia which was directly under their control. This militia was composed "of every able-bodied man" and for the most part each brought his own rifle. The fact that the common man was armed and willing to fight to protect their property and freedom was a serious miscalculation of the British Army. Noah's role in this was widespread and ultimately affected our Constitution, the Bill of Rights, and continues as a topic of heated discussion even today.

Noah served during the month of preparation, the actual fortifying of Dorchester Heights, and mustered out two weeks after the British evacuation – his papers dated at Roxbury, the command center for the entire effort. We don't know exactly what Noah did during these two months or the role he played on Dorchester Heights. Perhaps he was part of a rifle company or one of the workers hauling the fortifications up the hill and setting them in place. Whatever his individual role, we know that Noah Pratt volunteered and was part of both beginning and ending the siege of Boston. He witnessed the British withdrawal from the city and harbor. This common man helped make it happen. How many of us common people can lay claim to such a role in history? It gives me goose bumps just thinking about it.

Noah Pratt volunteered again in 1776 and was dispatched as part of "the northern army, company return dated at Fort Ticonderoga"[67]. This is the same area of fighting as the defeat and capture of the British army under Burgoyne a year later – which may well have been the turning point of France joining the Americans. This victory was once again possible because a large force of militia was brought up to unexpectedly cut off the British. By this time Noah had already been promoted as an officer in his regiment. Over the next few years his rank was respectfully noted in Wrentham birth records – to Lieutenant as daughter Sarah was born in 1779, and finally to Captain as daughter Susanna was born in 1781.[68] These promotions happened as the result of recommendations of his fellow officers, once again showing the respect he held among those who knew him. Still, through all my research there was no story of individual valor and in the end, Noah Pratt was just a common man who served his country at a time that it was needed.

---

66 *Massachusetts Soldiers and Sailors*, p708
67 Ibid p708
68 Massachusetts Vital Records 1600-1840: Wrentham

9 The Woodshop at Winchester

After the Revolution, the very first United States Census in 1790 records Noah and his family still living in Wrentham. However, a year later Noah Pratt and his wife sold their home and farm, and moved the entire family 95 miles northwest to a small town called Winchester NH. I should say the entire family except for their daughter Sarah who died

Figure 25: Sarah Pratt gravestone in Wrentham Cemetery, photo by Sue and Milt Bacheller

the previous year at the tender age of 12. Sarah was left alone buried in the cemetery back of Wrentham Meeting House. Noah had married, raised seven children, fought as a Minuteman, earned the respect of his neighbors, and attained the rank of Captain over 20 years living in Wrentham. In spite of that, no Pratt home has been found there and Sarah's lonely gravestone is perhaps the only visible proof that the family ever existed as part of Wrentham life.

What made Noah pack it all up and move to a remote town of 1,200 folks? Following the Revolution there was increased migration from the coastal areas moving inland. Not that long after there was migration all the way to Wisconsin in the Northwest Territory - on a recent ride I was surprised to find a small-town graveyard right here in Wisconsin with the grave of one of our Revolutionary veterans. Noah had some knowledge of Winchester NH because his older sister Olivia Pratt had moved there 20 years earlier with her husband William Humphrey and their family.[69] Both Olivia and her husband were dead by the time Noah relocated, so they were not the reason for the move. However, a footnote in history may give us a clue.

The same year Noah and his family moved to Winchester, the town voted to build a new meeting house and Noah was assigned to a committee of respected town leaders to "inspect the building site of said meeting-house and to have it completed within three years from this day". The committee of five men had all attained the respected rank of Lieutenant or higher in the Revolution.[70] That Capt. Noah Pratt would be assigned to

---

69 *Walking Back Through Time – 50 Historical Sketches of Winchester*, NH, Edith W Atkins, p66
70 *The History of Cheshire County, NH* p569 Minuets of Winchester Town Meeting October 1, 1792

this prestigious committee the same year he arrived in town shows a level of respect not commonly given a newcomer. Is it possible part of the reason Noah moved to Winchester in this time period was that he was chosen to build the new meeting house? Unfortunately, the meeting house built in 1794 burned to the ground in 1909 – so once again there is no evidence of Noah's hand in its construction.

There are also hints that perhaps Noah simply needed more space. In her charming historical tour through historic Winchester, Edith W. Atkins relates that "In 1792 Noah Pratt purchased 20 acres of land in Winchester on the south side of Mirey Brook with what is now Warwick Road passing through this virgin land. Noah, being of primitive spirit, wanted to make a home for his family, where he could both farm his land and carry on his trade as a cabinet maker. He built a two and one half story house on the right side of the road. A workshop was soon built on the opposite side of the road …. where he constructed furniture and cabinets for various people."[71]

Noah Pratt's home was built on Warwick Rd just east of Hy 10 going into Winchester. This home was timberframed just as Noah had built homes back in Wrentham, and a local historian "recalled an occupant telling me that there was a 1700's date carved in a beam in the attic".[72] You can imagine how sad I was to find Noah's home was neglected for decades and burned to the ground as a fire practice just six years prior to my search. How much I had hoped to match Noah's plane to some of the moulding still left in his home – again to no avail. We think about homes built 200 years ago by these patriots and wonder how they can be lost with such ease. However, if you let a house go just 30 years it can be ruined, and updating an old timberframe to modern living is difficult work. Unfortunately, not all of us are willing to come up with the time and money to preserve them. In spite of this, I hope there is still a home that Noah built standing somewhere waiting to be identified. Until that find, we are left without a single known example of Noah's work except for the cherry crown moulding plane that began my search for him. However, his firstborn son Henry was gifted in his work and we are lucky some of it has survived for us to see as a reflection of his father's teaching and their time working together.

The Pratt home and woodshop built in Winchester is the defining link between Noah the master woodworker, and his oldest son and apprentice, Henry Pratt. The 1790 Census shows Henry still living at home with his parents in Wrentham, so at age 19 he was not apprenticed and living with a master woodworker somewhere else. Now a young man of 21, Henry had learned the trade of woodworking at his father's bench in Wrentham even as the Revolution raged around them. Noah built the new family home with the help of his two oldest sons, and the shop was built for them to carry on the family business together. Noah passed the home and shop on to Henry when he died, and Henry continued his work in this woodshop over the course of 50 years. Even though the home and shop are gone, Henry is the window through which we can see their world.

---

71 *Walking Back Through Time – 50 Historical Sketches of Winchester*, NH, Edith W Atkins, p101
72 Letter from Edith W. Atkins, Feb 27, 1989

There are planes that have been found marked H. PRATT including some marked WRENTHAM.[73] Henry learned to make planes from Noah, along with how to build a home, cabinetmaking, farming, hunting, and everything else necessary to survive growing up in 18th century New England. Apprenticeship was really important in this time. It was the responsibility of parents not just to have their children educated, but to make sure they were taught something that would make them a contributing part of society. Even orphan children were placed into an apprenticeship or other arrangement to make certain they would not become a burden on the townsfolk. New Englanders were not as rigid about apprenticeship as in England, and there are many examples of fathers passing a trade on to their sons in this fashion.[74] It is sad how many parents shirk these basic responsibilities today.

In addition to Henry, Noah's second son Nathan likely worked at his father's bench because there are planes with his name as well. Noah's third son, finally a Noah Jr, was only 8 at the time they moved and he went on to become a physician – so we don't know how much help he was except for cleaning up the piles of shavings under the benches.

Figure 26: Author's woodshop, Autumn Woods Studio

We know quite a bit about Noah's woodshop from the probate listing when Henry passed away years later. Briefly, the estate listing for the shop included lots of lumber, 3 work benches, a turning lathe, 47 chisels, 19 bench planes and 64 moulding planes.[75] Clearly the shop was setup for business separate from the home and equipped for serious woodworking. The three benches were undoubtedly placed there for Noah, Henry, and Nathan. Most of the planes were probably made by them, and I believe Noah's cherry crown moulding plane was still sitting on the bench the day the shop and contents were sold in 1841.

Items like a veneer saw and a 'lot of gold leaf' lent themselves to fine furniture and not timberframing, so they were no longer focused on home building as a business. In addition to the usual shop tools, there were more curious items not so common, including a "lot of

73 *American Wooden Planes* 4th Edition, Thomas L Elliott, p329
74 *Early Planemakers of London,* Don & Anne Wing, p15
75 *New Hampshire Cheshire County Probate,* Henry Pratt Inventory Sept 21, 1841

organ pipes & patterns and 500 lbs of various pipe with 9 soddering irons". With nothing more than that, I did a simple internet search on PRATT + ORGAN and learned that Henry Pratt was one of our earliest organ makers earning him a small place in our country's early history. Through Henry and his organs I learned so much more about Noah and their work together.

There is a story that Henry accompanied his father to Hudson NY to install an organ in a church.[76] This is amazing, because by today's roads, Hudson is 128 miles from Winchester NH. It certainly would have been easier to bring someone from one of the big cities like Springfield or Albany to do the work. Clearly Noah Pratt had enough of a reputation for the quality of his work that someone sought him out for this task. The story continues that Henry, being a musician in his own right, took great interest in the project and soon afterward launched plans to build an organ himself. (Yes, by all means, let's just build an organ.) As he worked, one of the church members offered Henry a bushel of rye every day until the organ was finished – and to pay Henry $300 for the organ if it would play.

Let's put this in perspective. In 1790 there were only a handful of organs in all of Boston and none in the Congregational churches scattered throughout New England. Most people in New England had never even seen an organ or heard one play, and the Puritans that dominated the region had not yet accepted organ music as a proper part of church worship. Into this setting a young man with no real experience decides to build an organ in a small rural community – and changes everything! Certainly Henry could build something that looked like an organ, but his ability to actually get it to play was far from certain. However, in 1799 the church member indeed paid Henry for the completed organ and donated it to the Winchester Congregational Church. We know the organ played because, incredibly, Henry's first organ still exists today on the second floor of the Winchester NH Library in fine playing condition. This is the oldest organ made in New England that has survived for us today[77] and the people of Winchester have done a remarkable job of preserving it for us to enjoy.

Building this organ was not some frivolous pastime for Henry because by this time he was married with three children of his own. Even so, Henry completed this first organ under the watchful eye of his father in their woodshop in Winchester. The two of them had worked together in Wrentham since Henry was a small boy, and he was now a mature woodworker 28 years old. I have no doubt that the organ building genius was all Henry's. But as I look at the first organ Henry made, it is clear that his furniture skills came from Noah. His first organ shows how early in his career Henry was already a consummate cabinet maker.

---

76 *Walking Back Through Time – 50 Historical Sketches of Winchester*, NH, Edith W Atkins, p102
77 www.rhedgebeth.com/opuslist.htm

Figure 27: Henry Pratt Opus 1, built in 1799
Conant Library Historical Department, Winchester NH

Pictured here is Henry Pratt's Opus 1 (first work) as seen today in Winchester NH. The case is made of old growth white pine and faux grained to look like mahogany, a common practice of the time. It is 10 foot tall and modest in appearance except for the gilt pipes. These are just for show, turned on a wood lathe and finished with gold leaf – both of which were in the woodshop estate inventory mentioned earlier. The real organ pipes are behind these, the larger ones made of wood, and others made of lead sheet taken from tea chests arriving from the China trade in Boston.[78] The bellows used to pump air to the pipes has a hand lever on the side of the organ.

The white pine case is made with frame & panel construction. This basic construction method still used today would have torn itself apart over the course of 200 years of heat and cold if Henry had not known his trade. The real clue to his craftsmanship though is the keyboard, an absolute jewel shown here in more detail.

Figure 28: Henry Pratt Opus 1 keyboard detail

The keys are veneered in beautiful mahogany with ivory inlay, and the moulding details are quite elegant. This first keyboard exhibits Henry's craftsmanship at an early stage and shows the extent of his father's teaching, including wood turning, veneer work, inlay, and a fine eye for beautiful details.

---

78 Organ Building in New England, New England Magazine 1834, p210

In addition to church organs, Henry also made smaller parlor organs for use in people's homes. The Winchester Library has one of these that puts an end to any thought Henry was a small town country woodworker only capable of primitive furniture. The organ shown here is his sixth work – still very early in his career. This work was not restrained by the modest requirements of his church, and he used beautifully figured bookmatched mahogany for the case.

Figure 29: Henry Pratt parlor organ, Conant Library Historical Department, Winchester NH

The panel above the keyboard is birdseye maple with an inset brass plate engraved *Henry Pratt, Winchester NH*. While I might have chosen a different fabric to cover the pipes, I suspect the restoration of the organ included fabric that was representative of the period. Viewed just as a piece of furniture, this organ was high style for a rural home in the early 1800s and unusually fine work considering it was made in Winchester NH and not Boston or Newport.

In traveling to see Henry Pratt's organs, the one with the most profound effect on me is in the Memorial Hall Museum at Historic Deerfield in Massachusetts. Deerfield Academy built this brick school building in 1798 about the time that Henry began building organs. By 1880 this building became one of the first museums in New England, and today the entire village is a walking museum. Their organ was made for Rev. Preserved Smith who preached in Deerfield. Rev. Smith's widow gifted the organ to the museum in 1883 shortly after it was founded, so the provenance is impeccable.

Figure 30: Author with Henry Pratt plane and parlor organ c1820 at Memorial Hall Museum, Deerfield Mass

Memorial Hall's organ, shown here with the author, was crafted by Henry circa 1820 - about half way through his career - and is a mature statement of his skill. The case is solid cherry with four beautifully bookmatched figured panels in the doors covering the organ pipes. Henry's work includes a painted floral panel over the keyboard, a pierced work bonnet, and turned finials once again demonstrating the use of his lathe in the woodshop. Memorial Hall Museum indicates this is the only parlor organ left with Henry's original keyboard, and it is almost identical to his Opus 1 back in Winchester.

Viewed as a piece of furniture, this organ struck a very personal chord because of its close relationship to my own work. The form of Henry's cabinet is relatively simple except for the pierced bonnet, but he used especially beautiful wood in the doors to great effect. To accomplish this, Henry resawed the four bookmatched upper door panels from a single thick - highly figured piece of cherry crotch wood. Henry, or perhaps even Noah, picked this piece of wood as something special and set it aside to dry in the woodshop for a period of years, waiting for a project such as this to come along.

As if this organ wasn't already special enough to me, there was something even more profound we discovered. A couple of years earlier I managed to purchase one of Henry Pratt's planes. Incredibly, this was the very plane used by Henry to make the top moulding on this organ. In this picture you can see the organ moulding and the plane that made the moulding almost 200 years ago, and you can see the H.PRATT mark upside-down on the front of the plane. Henry's plane is made of cherry, perhaps even the same wood used to make this organ. You cannot imagine the

goosebumps over our discovery, and my wife Dee and I celebrated with a fine dinner and wine at the Deerfield Inn that evening.

Over the years, Henry is estimated to have built 50-70 organs, although very few identified with his making are left. Many of these were the first organs in small Congregational Churches scattered throughout New England. As such, Henry Pratt played a modest role in convincing these Puritan descendants that song accompanied by organ music was appropriate praise to God. There is an article from the New England Magazine published in 1834 on "Organ Building in New-England" whose author actually corresponded with Henry Pratt – may even have met him – listing organs he built including one for his hometown congregation of Wrentham. This would have been their first organ around 1802-06 and it is likely Noah helped Henry deliver and install it. Can we imagine the Wrentham congregation gathered for the first time to hear this wondrous sound swelling to the heavens, and how proud Noah was of Henry and his work?

The Wrentham organ happened late in life for Noah, for he died Jan 4, 1807 at the age of 59. I have this picture of Noah Pratt in death going up to the pearly gates and St. Peter asks him "Well, Noah, what did you do with your life?" Noah answers "I was a woodworker – I built homes, furniture, made a few planes along the way. I never got the chance to build an ark – but I helped build a nation". Noah is buried on a quiet hillside in Evergreen Cemetery in Winchester surrounded by his family and a few lonely trees. His gravestone shows the respect of his family and country, and a rather lengthy inscription that reads:

Capt
Noah Pratt died
Jan 4th 1807 aged 59

Why do ye friends repine
Since all memories are o'er
Rejoice that we thro' grace devine
Shall meet to part no more
Some hearty friend shall drop a heart
O'er these dry bones + lay
(And perhaps there was a bit more,
But it's not there for us to see today)

Figure 31: Noah Pratt gravestone in Evergreen Cemetery, Winchester NH, photo by Sue and Milt Bacheller

Henry was still building organs in their woodshop at age 69, including one that may have been his last that was delivered via the Erie Canal all the way to St. Patrick's church in Largo, Indiana.[79] Henry died in Winchester in 1841 and is buried in Evergreen Cemetery along with Noah and their extended families. By this time our country was covered with factories of every shape and size manufacturing every conceivable product – including organs. The age of individually hand-crafted organs was gone. Although Henry's son Julius repaired Opus 1 in 1840, in the end no one carried on the woodworking or organ building tradition in Henry's family.

Henry died a successful and respected man. His position in life is reflected in his estate of almost $4,000. In spite of his success, Henry owed $800 more than his cash on hand, and this forced the sale of his land and home to settle the estate. I suppose this is the quintessential argument for life insurance. This also brings into view a practice quite foreign to our modern experience. While the farm and home were sold, Henry's widow Rebecca was granted a dower of 1/3 of the farm and home to live her life out. Probate is quite clear in granting her one of the bedrooms and privilege of the hallway, stairs and kitchen. Rebecca also got acres of apple trees and woodlot, and kept many of the family possessions. Can we even begin to imagine buying a farm today and having to share a third of the house with the widow Pratt for the rest of her days? This was their answer to caring for people without providing a welfare system.

*So ends the story of Noah Pratt, his son Henry,
and their time together in the woodshop.*

---

79 *Unnamed newspaper clipping,* Largo IN, 11/12/04, edited by Nicole Hahn

10   Other Planemakers Who Served

My story has focused on Noah Pratt's service in the Revolution because it was his plane that set me on this journey. However, there are a small number of other planemakers that are known to have served in the Revolutionary War. In this chapter I would like to mention some of them and share their story with you.

★ ★ ★   Lexington & Concord   ★ ★ ★

John Walton Jr of Reading Massachusetts was born in 1710 and was a housewright, joiner, and planemaker just like Noah Pratt. He also served as a lumber surveyor and tax assessor for the town.[80] On April 19, 1775 the town of Reading sent four companies to join the fight that was raging at Lexington and Concord. One of the Reading companies was led by

Figure 32: Plane made by Capt. John Walton Jr marked IN+READING, author's collection, photo by Bob Poull

Capt. John Walton Jr who was 65 years of age[81] and marched 18 miles to reach Concord – a distance equal to what the British had marched to that point. John Jr was the perfect example of the militia's definition of "every able-bodied man" that was expected to serve. John earned his position of command having already served in the French and Indian Wars. John's company of 88 men reached Meriam's Corner about the same time as the British force about a mile south of Concord on their retreat back to Boston. The British had just rested some hours in Concord, but John Walton and his men marched right into the fight without a stop. There were four other Waltons in John's company, and two of John's sons fought that day in other companies listed below. John was an early planemaker in the region and apparently made planes until his death in 1785, just a few short years after the Revolution was won.

John Walton's son Benjamin (also of Reading Mass) marched with the company of Capt John Bacheler, reaching the fight at the same time and place and fought alongside his father's company. Benjamin was a housewright and planemaker in his own right.

---

80   *American Wooden Planes* by Emil & Martyl Pollak, 4th Edition Revised by Thomas L. Elliott, p427
81   *The Battle of April 19 1775* by Frank Warren Coburn, p96- 97

Benjamin served throughout the Revolutionary War and went on to serve as a Lieutenant in the War of 1812.[82]

John Walton's oldest son John III fought that day as a Lieutenant second in command in Capt Samuel Thatcher's company from Cambridge Mass. [83] Thatcher's company joined the fight at Lincoln alongside the Lexington Company as they re-joined the battle after their initial skirmish early that morning. John III and his brother Benjamin were partners in planemaking, and John had moved to Cambridge in 1771 working as a housewright.

Samuel Doggett Jr was born in 1751 and worked as a millwright, housewright, and planemaker following in his father's footsteps as was so often the case.[84] Samuel Jr was a Minuteman and marched from Dedham Massachusetts in Capt Aaron Fuller's company of 67 men. They marched 20 miles and joined the fight at Arlington sometime after John Walton's men joined the fight. Lord Percy's reinforcements had already joined the main British force and begun pillaging and burning homes along their retreat through Arlington, so the fighting here was fierce.[85] Samuel continued making planes after the war, and was awarded a pension in 1818 for service to his country.

Quite recently a fifth planemaker has been identified[86] who fought at the Battle of Lexington and Concord. Joseph Gould was born in 1730 and served as an apprentice to John Walton Jr, completing his training in 1751. Joseph was a joiner, wheelwright, and made handplanes with his name on them. It should come as no surprise that Joseph also marched in Capt John Walton Jr's company to Concord, covered in detail above. Just in the last few paragraphs, do you get the feel of how tightly woven the people in these towns were? Through the years, Joseph kept a pair of leather-bound ledgers of his work currently conserved by *Historic New England*.

Figure 33: Plane by S Doggett Jr marked DEDHAM, author's collection, photo by Bob Poull

82   *American Wooden Planes* by Emil & Martyl Pollak, 4th Edition Revised by Thomas L. Elliott, p427
83   *The Battle of April 19 1775* by Frank Warren Coburn, Muster Roll, p41
84   *American Wooden Planes* by Emil & Martyl Pollak, 4th Edition Revised by Thomas L. Elliott, p125
85   *The Battle of April 19 1775* by Frank Warren Coburn, p133, 134
86   *Joseph Gould, Planemaker, a Patriot of the Battle of Lexington and Concord*, by Thomas Elliott in EAIA Chronicle Vol 62 No 1 p35

★ ★ ★ Bunker Hill ★ ★ ★

The Battle of Bunker Hill was covered in some detail back in chapter 6. John Sleeper was one of the men who fought for our freedom at Bunker Hill. John was born August 2, 1754, the son of Henry Sleeper, a renowned cabinetmaker in Newburyport Massachusetts just north of Boston. John was a cabinetmaker and an important planemaker of the period.[87] Newburyport was a busy port and shipbuilding center in 1775, but certainly existed 'in the shadow' of Boston. A local resident wrote "Let it be remembered that British tea was destroyed in Newburyport a week or ten days before the event of a like nature in Boston; but Market square (Newburyport) is a much humbler locality than Boston Harbor, and so the trumpet of Fame has been silent over it."[88]

Just like Noah Pratt, John Sleeper and his company responded to the call at Lexington & Concord but arrived too late to fight that day. However, John Sleeper and 58 of his townsfolk volunteered on May 2, 1775 and joined Colonel Moses Little's Regiment. [89] Little's regiment marched to Cambridge headquarters arriving May 12th, and was with the men that defended the main fort and breastwork at Bunker Hill. Another group of this regiment manned an unfortified road down to Charlestown that strafed the British as they attacked the fort.[90] Covering their final retreat, there "were also small groups consisted of Gardner's and Little's regiments that formed up behind a low, thin stone wall and traded volleys for several minutes with three British light companies, before withdrawing fence by fence to the Neck, leaving the regulars with heavy losses"[91] and saving many American lives

John Sleeper's older brother Moses kept a diary that is in the archives at the Longfellow National Historic site in Cambridge, Massachusetts. Moses also served in Little's regiment, although a different company then brother John. One entry by Moses mentions: *"Wednesday August 2 this day dind with Brother John It being his Birth Day and 21 years old this day"*.[92] Moses was only 23 and focused more on the family cabinetmaking trade. How uncanny to read of such a personal meal shared by two young brothers at such a precarious point in their life and our country's history.

Following his service at Bunker Hill, John Sleeper was also one of about 20 Newburyport men that volunteered "in the expedition under Montgomery, which went up through the woods to Quebec, suffering severely. Upon the death of Montgomery, John Sleeper was taken prisoner, and lay in prison nine months." Here is a successful planemaker that could

---

87 *American Wooden Planes* by Emil & Martyl Pollak, 4th Edition Revised by Thomas L. Elliott, p375
88 *Historical Society of Old Newbury* contributed by Miss E. A. Getchell April 1894
89 *Massachusetts Soldiers and Sailors in the War of the Revolution*, p295
90 *Decisive Day – The Battle for Bunker Hill* by Richard M. Ketchum, p146
91 *Boston 1775 – The Shot Heard Around the World* by Brendan Morrissey, p65
92 *"Who Wrote the Soldier's Diary"* by Frances Dickinson Ackerly on *www.longfellowfriends.org/journal/diaryintro.pdf*

have chosen to stay home. How strong his belief in freedom must have been, because even following his imprisonment, he volunteered further as "ships carpenter in the frigate Boston".[93]

In a letter from Samuel Adams attending the Continental Congress in Philadelphia on Dec 22 1775 to John Adams, Samuel wrote *"I know it give you great Pleasure to be informed that this Congress have ordered the Building of thirteen Ships of War, five with 32 guns, five of 28 and three of 24. Our Colony (Massachusetts) is to build two of these Ships".[94]* These were our first commissioned warships – the very genesis of the United States Navy.

Figure 34: Frigate Boston, painting by Rod Claudius in 1962, official U.S. Navy photo compliments of www.history.navy.mil

The Continental Frigate *Boston* shown above was one of these first thirteen ships, a 514-ton 24-gun frigate built right there in Newburyport as part of the effort by the American colonies to create a seagoing navy. John Sleeper was right there to see the keel laid in 1776 – may have even worked on the ship as it was built. Completed in 1777, in May of that year she began a North Atlantic cruise in company with the frigate *Hancock*. In addition to making prizes of two merchant vessels, they captured the British 28-gun frigate *Fox* on 7 June. A month later, *Boston* was able to escape when *Hancock* and *Fox* were taken by a stronger enemy squadron.

---

93 *History of Chester NH* by Benjamin Chase as referenced in American Wooden Planes, p 375
94 *Navel Documents of the American Revolution* ed William Bell Clark for USN V3, p 209

In February and March 1778 she transported American envoy John Adams to France, then remained in European waters raiding British commerce. She returned to the Colonies in October. The following year *Boston* operated in the North Atlantic, taking several prizes while sailing in July-September and November-December. In 1780 she took part in the defense of Charleston, South Carolina, and was captured there by the British on May 12th. John was one of the most prolific of our early American planemakers, so his planes are relatively easy to find – but still one in a million. Early one autumn morning at my

hometown flea market my wife picked up a plane to show me – and my heart almost stopped as I recognized the I.SLEEPER mark on the toe. Her find brought me to a group of six planes in a barn here in Wisconsin – two of them Sleeper's, three made by David Hunkins of Haverhill Massachusetts nearby, and a small beauty that was unmarked. These planes were clearly made in the last quarter of the 1700s. Historians tell us that many of the earliest settlers of Wisconsin in the early 1800s

Figure 35: Six planes found together in Wisconsin, all late 1700's. Third from left and far right are by John Sleeper. Author's collection, photo by Bob Poull

were "Yankees" from New England looking for new land and the native forest that was so rich here. These planes certainly meant something to the woodworker that carried them all the way from Massachusetts to the Wisconsin Territory. I suspect following his use building the original homestead, passing generations relegated them to the barn where they deteriorated waiting for me to claim them. How lucky I am that they were not discarded as junk or burned given their poor condition.

The diamond shaped 'strike' button in front of the iron (plane at right) was provided to cushion the blow of a mallet as the user loosened the iron to sharpen or readjust it. Sleeper's diamond shaped strike is made of rosewood - a signature of his own making.

What an understatement to say that John Sleeper lived a full life. After the war he continued making planes in Newburyport, moving to Chester NH and died there in 1834 at the age of 80. In his will he described himself simply as a planemaker. I wonder how many of us could stand up to his measure of a common citizen of our country.

★ ★ ★ Washington Crossing the Delaware ★ ★ ★

When General Washington evicted the British from Boston (with a little help from Noah Pratt on Dorchester Heights), he already knew the British would most likely re-locate in New York City. New York was much more loyalist than Boston and would be more difficult for Washington to defend. Regardless he did pitch a strong defense but got outmaneuvered twice, at Long Island and New York City. What should have been a crushing defeat was softened by the fact he was miraculously able to slip away with the whole of his army to continue the war. This was a very difficult time for Washington and the colonies, only a few short months after our proud Declaration of Independence. While still on the defense, Washington's decision to cross the Delaware River that Christmas night of 1776 was a stroke of genius. If the British had been told Washington would cross the river that night, they would not have believed it possible. Washington crossed the river in the dead of night, in small boats with treacherous ice on the river in the midst of a ferocious storm. The weather was so bitter that two American soldiers froze to death on the march to Trenton that night.

Figure 36: Art print of Washington Crossing the Delaware. Original painting by Emanuel Leutze 1851 located at Metropolitan Museum of Art, New York City

Amongst the men that made that brave river crossing with Washington was John Lindenberger. John was born in 1754 and worked as a cabinetmaker and joiner in Baltimore MD. John's father had emigrated from Germany, so John joined the "German Regiment" led by Col Nicholas Haussegger[95] to fight for the colonies. It was good that John and his German regiment were present considering the bulk of the troops in Trenton were Hessians hired from Germany to fight for the British. The surprise attack was complete and over 900 Hessians surrendered without a single American casualty. Washington pulled the exact same move a week later and surprised the British force at Princeton – and once again John Lindenberger was there. At least one report says that Lieut John Lindenberger, a cabinetmaker by trade, led the force that escorted the Hessian prisoners to safe keeping in Baltimore.[96]

John went on to serve with the 4th Continental Artillery of Pennsylvania the next year and fought in the Battles of Brandywine and Germantown. While in the artillery it's reasonable to assume he met William Martin, a planemaker from Philadelphia serving in the same unit - mentioned below. John resigned his commission with the army in March of 1778 for reasons unknown, and we lose track of him until record of his marriage in 1785 on the outskirts of Providence RI. Somewhere in those seven years, John learned the trade of planemaking, perhaps in Philadelphia from William Martin (mentioned below).

Figure 37: Advertisement reported in Plane Talk Fall 1989, courtesy of Astragal Press

Within two years of his marriage, John moved his family and business into Providence RI, as seen in the *United States Chronicle* advertisement from June 14, 1787 at left. In addition to cabinetmaking, John went on to be a prolific planemaker, blacksmith, toolmaker, and taught architecture. John had much success in his business dealings and continued planemaking till he died in 1817, but alas his estate was insolvent as was so often the case with our early planemakers.

I have seen a number of John Lindenberger's planes in exotic hardwoods, which he had ready access to considering Providence was a busy seaport.

95 *John Lindenberger and his Descendants* by Anne and Donald Wing, Plane Talk Fall 1989 p186, Astragal Press
96 *German Allied Troops in the North American War of Independence* by Max Von Eelking 1893 English Translation p81

The plane shown here is made of baywood (Persea borbonia, redbay, sweetbay) that probably came on a ship from along the Atlantic coast or the Bahamas which New England traded with extensively. I learned this wood "was used for high-quality furniture before mahogany came into general use in the United States".[97] Remember, John was trained as a cabinetmaker by his father. The wood of this plane has an almost overpowering scent even 200 years after it was made. Just think, here is a plane made by a man who crossed the Delaware with Gen George Washington on Christmas in 1776.

Figure 38: Plane by John Lindenberger (above). Photo at left shows maker's mark with Old English I as first initial for John. Author's collection, photos by Bob Poull

★   ★   ★   ★   ★

Jo Fuller was born in 1746 and worked in Providence RI as one of our most important early planemakers. We know that Jo Fuller served as an officer during the Revolution and was also a deacon of his church.[98] In December of 1776 Jo was an Ensign in the 4th Company of Providence Militia and eventually reached the rank of Captain. He was second in command of his company at the Battle of Rohde Island in 1778.[99] This battle to evict the British from their occupation of Newport RI was the first attempt to coordinate Continental and French forces including the French fleet. Our Continental troops were supplemented by militia called up for the campaign, including Jo Fuller's company and the 1st Rhode Island, the first black regiment in America's history.

---

97   *A Guide to Useful Woods of the World*, edited by James H. Flynn, Jr and Charles D. Holder, p405
98   *American Wooden Planes* by Emil & Martyl Pollak, 4th Edition Revised by Thomas L. Elliott, p158
99   *From the Mechanic's Workbench* by Don & Anne Wing, date unknown

Born in Connecticut, Jo Fuller is first noted in Providence by advertisement in the *Providence Gazette* in Dec of 1772 announcing "joiners tools made and sold by Joseph Fuller". While still not commonly found, the quantity and quality of Jo Fuller's planes indicate he earned most of his living as a planemaker. Living in the heart of a city like Providence, it is likely that Jo Fuller did not have to farm as part of his subsistence like Noah Pratt and many of the other rural planemakers. There are also documented a number of other important planemakers that learned the trade as an apprentice to Jo Fuller, so his influence was widely felt. Jo was a charter member of the Providence Association of Mechanics and Manufacturers in 1789. Unusual for the time, there is no record of Jo Fuller having any natural-born children. Perhaps as a result of this, Jo adopted one of his apprentices by the name of Joseph Field in 1791, who then took the name Joseph Fuller, Jr.

Jo Fuller started making planes just before the Revolution, about the same timeframe as Noah Pratt. To me this period was the "gold standard" of planes made with more care and detail to the point of pure art. The moulding plane shown here is from this period. Note the decorative "fluting" at the bottom of the chamfers on the edge of the moulding plane. This is described further in Appendix A and is more properly called a lamb's tongue, a detail used on timber framed posts more so in England than in the colonies. Our planemakers were familiar with it and it somehow crept into plane making at least in New England for a brief period surrounding the Revolution. Jo Fuller is also unique in an unusual maker's mark he used that included a USA stamp[100], perhaps one of the first instances of someone marking their work with the new country designation they were so proud of.

Figure 39: (above) Plane marked JO,FULLER and PROVIDENCE. Author's collection, photo by Bob Poull. (at right) Fuller mark with USA.

100 *American Wooden Planes* by Emil & Martyl Pollak, 4th Edition Revised by Thomas L. Elliott, p159

★ ★ ★ ★ ★

William Martin worked as a planemaker 1773 to 1801 in Philadelphia PA. Both William Martin and John Lindenberger (mentioned earlier) served as first lieutenants in the 4th Continental Artillery, enlisting three weeks apart in 1777 and served in the New Jersey campaign.[101] Most certainly these two knew each other, leading to the speculation that John apprenticed to William to learn the trade of planemaking sometime after their service together. Once again, there has been little research on William Martin, but there is this wonderful window into these people and the times reported in one of the local newspapers of a Grand Federal Procession on July 4, 1788.[102] This parade and celebration was honoring the Declaration of Independence signed on this date in 1776 and the "establishment of the Constitution or Frame of Government". Our Constitution had been drafted just the previous September right there in Philadelphia and was already ratified by Pennsylvania and nine other states even as this parade wound through the streets of our nation's capitol. The newspaper reports that military companies, the trades, and professions were represented in this festive parade. Some distance behind the contingent of four hundred and fifty architects and house carpenters came the planemakers, led by William Martin "bearing the standard with white field, a smoothing plane on the top; a pair of spring dividers, three planes; a brace and square." Now there was a 4th of July parade I should have liked to ride in!

Shown here is a massive crown moulding plane made by William Martin. This plane is made of beech and perhaps you can sense it looks quite different, lacking any artistic refinement compared to many of the planes previously shown here. The planemakers in Philadelphia worked more in the style of the British makers and were not influenced by the work we have studied in and around Wrentham and Providence just 300 miles away.

Figure 40: (above) Crown moulding plane by William Martin of Philadelphia. (at left) Makers mark on the toe of the plane WMARTIN PHILAD and 6 ½ in reference to the width of the moulding produced by this massive plane. Author's collection, photo by Bob Poull

---

101 *Eighteenth-Century Woodworking Tools* edited by James M. Gaynor, paper presented by Donald and Anne Wing
102 *American Woodworking Tools* by Paul B Kababian and Dudley Wilney, p85

★　★　★　★　★

By your leave, I would like to include a plane here made by an unknown maker with the mark of GxP where the x is used in place of a period. The plane shown here is a gunstock plane, one of the least common planes to be found. These planes were used by gun makers to groove the top of the long gunstock to hold the gun barrel and protect the users hand from the extreme heat of repeated firing. This plane is most certainly of the Revolutionary era and from the same portion of New England we've studied around Wrentham. A close examination shows the wedge and fluting are certainly in the style of Jo Fuller of Providence. A reference to the arms makers of the period shows the Peck family in Providence, with Elihu Peck as a gunstocker and armorer.[103] Checking the name Peck in *American Planes* shows planemakers by the name in Rehoboth Massachusetts next door to Providence. Perhaps someday we will learn who G.P was and more about his life. It is worth taking a moment to dwell on the fact that whoever used this plane was certainly making guns used by our patriots fighting in the Revolution.

Figure 41: Plane used to make gunstocks marked only GxP. Note the lambs-tongue under the chamfer done in the style of Jo Fuller seen earlier. Author's collection, photo by Bob Poull

★　★　★　★　★

The last two planemakers from the New England area that I will mention both died for our freedom while serving in the Revolution. You can imagine that planes from either of these men are quite rare, and I do not have samples that I can share with you.

Nathaniel Briggs (b. 1744, d. 1777) was part of the Massachusetts and NH militia called up in the summer of 1777 to help stop Burgoyne's campaign to split our country in half with his force coming down from the north. The militia played a key role in cutting off Burgoyne from his supplies and forcing the surrender of the entire British force, and ultimately provided reason for the French to join the colonies in our fight for freedom. Nathaniel died from wounds received in the Battle of Bennington.

---

103 *Arms Makers of Colonial America*, James B Whisker, p144

John Holt (b.1746, d. 1781) was a cabinetmaker from New London CT, home to many of the privately owned armed ships that preyed on British supply shipping throughout the war. Late in the summer of 1781 the British sent a force to put an end to this menace with the British commander no less than our notorious traitor, Benedict Arnold. The British caught them by surprise, and immediately burned almost all of New London to the ground. Fighting was particularly fierce at Fort Griswold across the river from New London, and John Holt is one of those killed in this fight.

★　★　★　★　★

We do not have paintings of these planemaker patriots – all of them being common men as they were. However, here is what we have to remember them as a group of soldiers standing in a row, proud of their place in our American history. Perhaps we could give them a moment of silence and respect which they so richly deserve.

Figure 42: Planemakers who served in the American Revolution - from left William Martin, John Sleeper, John Walton, John Lindenberger, Jo Fuller, Samuel Doggett, unknown, and Noah Pratt. Author's collection, photo by Bob Poull

11   Revolution

As we come to the end of my story, it is early summer and I find myself torn between riding and writing this chapter. Oh, how often we must strike a balance with the things we want in life. We have been 10-20 degrees below normal temperature for most of the last month. When it should be 75 at mid-day and all you scratch out is 55, it feels more like April than June. Once again, no sign of global warming here. So, I find myself doing more writing than riding, and I've been musing over what I've written and how to say what is left to be said.

While searching for Noah Pratt and insight to his life, I stumbled on one of those rare instances where a legal document opens a window and sheds some light on the real person. When Noah and his wife Hannah sold their home and farm in Wrentham, the hand written deed of sale was dated

> ### *"the twenty fourth day of December in the year of our Lord 1791 – and in the sixteenth year of the Independence of the United States of America".*[104]

Ten years had gone by since the end of the Revolution, but the new car smell had not worn off. They still reveled in hearing it – took every opportunity to say it again – "the Independence of the United States of America". Remember William Martin who "bore the standard of the planemakers in the Fourth of July Grand Procession of 1788 in Philadelphia – an important annual ceremony in the early days of our Republic".[105] How

important freedom was to these people - the extent to which freedom permeated their lives. As I read more about the Revolution and the planemakers, and even more so as I wrote – I felt an overwhelming inner need to balance what I learned against our own life, our current times and experience. I wonder if we really appreciate what they did for us - do we celebrate our freedom with the same passion? Do we understand what freedom is – really? How well have we preserved and grown the freedom that was given to us by these common folk?

While preparing for one of my research trips to Boston, I called a hotel where I planned to stay to

---

104 *Wrentham records*, Book 174 Page 197.
105 *American Wooden Planes* by Emil & Martyl Pollak, 4th Edition Revised by Thomas L. Elliott, p268

ask how close they were to Bunker Hill. The young lady at the desk seemed confused, and then asked me what that was – the mall? The hotel turned out to be across the street from historic Charlestown that was burned by the British as they attacked Bunker Hill just a few blocks away – and this person didn't even know what Bunker Hill was, much less the significance of the men who died there. I fear we've reached the point where we are more familiar with the history of Star Wars than our own Revolutionary War. There's a good chance this young lady could tell me Luke Skywalker's life story, but perhaps nothing about Paul Revere. Beyond such ignorance of our history, I fear there is an even broader apathy about how well we are managing our freedom today.

Ultimately our fight for freedom was to take the power of government from the Crown for our own. This freedom for "we the people" to govern ourselves – to collectively vote and decide what government means - is real power wielded by each individual citizen – every one of us. Spider Man's father-figure uncle Ben is fond of saying "with great power comes great responsibility". Truth is, our collective responsibility to wield the power of freedom has not always been well used. You may have noticed that I have been pretty upbeat in my portrayal of the Revolution, as most of our history books have done in the past. I am really impressed with the "miracle" quality of the first year of the war which has been the relatively narrow topic of my story. However, I am sure we realize our Revolution was not perfect and left some important business undone. Some of this has been left festering like an open wound until our own lifetime, and today the residual effects are still being felt over two centuries after we won our freedom.

When our founding fathers declared that "all men were created equal" they really meant "all white men" and they most certainly did not mean to include their women in these rights. Even as we have built this amazing country founded on democracy, we have shown a persistent and pervasive willingness of the majority to force our collective will on others in order to build and maintain a position of power and wealth. Our history books have left us an image so whitewashed of the truth that we are able to look down our nose at other people of the world, pointing at their record of human rights, ethnic cleansing, and genocide while being totally oblivious to our own past. When any example of this is raised, our whitewashed answer is "that was a different time, that's just the way they did it back then, there were reasons for that, and anyhow someone else did it – not me or my people". My belief in the importance of history is; if we don't know where we've been, perhaps we'll wind up there again. So, allow me to briefly put some of this unfinished business in perspective.

★   ★   ★   ★   ★

Slavery was part of America from our earliest colonization. Southern tobacco and cotton plantations were made profitable with the use of large numbers of slaves. However, Francis Nicholson of Wrentham Massachusetts had a slave – remember Cesar Chelor, the black planemaker mentioned earlier? I was surprised to learn the extent to which slavery also existed in the north. There were calls to end slavery long before the Revolution – but there was still a slave market in Boston as late as 1761. We know this because our first black American poet, Phillis Wheatley, was sold as a young girl in the Boston slave market that year. Phillis gained international acclaim, and a poem she wrote to General Washington during the siege of Boston prompted him to write a letter to her complimenting her prose.[106] Slavery was not just a southern problem. In addition to widespread slavery in the north, the vast majority of slave trading was done by northern ship owners and captains – and whole towns grew wealthy building ships and outfitting the slave trade.[107] If you read *Inheriting the Trade* written by a direct descendant of one of these slave traders, you will realize that this slave trade was even more horrific and inhumane then most slave life on southern plantations.

Many blacks fought valiantly to win our freedom in the Revolution. Remember Prince Estabrook "a man of color" mentioned earlier among the first killed and wounded at Lexington?[108] Another black, Salem Prince, fought fearlessly at Bunker Hill and is memorialized in Jonathan Trumbull's famous painting of the battle. Even though 5,000 blacks served in the Continental Army, we did not end the horrors of slavery until the Civil War a hundred years later. Yet another hundred years passed and our country went through a huge upheaval in the 1960s to realize we still had not provided minorities with the most basic rights promised in the Declaration, Constitution, and Bill of rights. In my own lifetime northern hotels refused "darkies" a room, and lynch mobs that hung blacks without due process and without recrimination were still common in many parts of our country. Since then we have gone through huge effort and expense to realize the promise that all men are created equal. Many blacks have worked hard to take their place in every position of society, even now including our President Barack Obama. This historic election was not possible without a large portion of our white population casting their vote in a way that would not have happened just 40 years ago. But I was still shocked to hear white people say they could never vote for Barack Obama simply because he was black. With all our progress, there is still much work to be done.

★   ★   ★   ★   ★

When we arrived in this "new world" it was only new to us. Native American people occupied most of our country as we arrived to claim this land for England, France, Spain, or whatever other country thought they had a right to it. As a young child I remember playing cowboys and Indians. I remember Indians had bows and arrows, and cowboys had guns. I never questioned what happened to all those Indians as I learned in grade school about "manifest destiny", this God given right for our young country to settle the Northwest Territory, and Louisiana, and then sweeping through the west until we controlled the entire land "from sea to shining sea". It wasn't till later while reading *Bury my Heart at Wounded Knee* that I began to sense the horrors that our history books had left out. In truth, we systematically begged, borrowed, and stole this land from the Indians right from the start.

106 *1776* by David McCullough, p 90
107 *Inheriting the Trade* by Thomas Norman DeWolf, pxiii
108 *The Battle of April 19 1775* by Frank Warren Coburn, p 70

We reveled in the stories of trading Manhattan for a boxful of baubles, bangles, and bright shinny beads. The Puritans in Massachusetts (who I've been very respectful of thus far) reportedly enacted early laws that Indians who didn't accept their faith were put to death for blasphemy. Throughout the colonies Indians were captured, enslaved, and sold into exile. From 1670 to 1715 between 30-50,000 Native Americans were exported from the colonies against their will. [109]

Few of us realize that our Revolution was not just fought over freedom. It was also fomented by influential men who hoped to get rich speculating on western land. Did you know that the original charter for the Massachusetts Bay Colony legally extended their border westward to the Pacific Ocean?[110] Maps of the period like the one below often show the colonies of Massachusetts, Virginia, and the Carolinas with no western border at all – the colonies were drawn far out to the west.

Figure 43: A Map of British and French settlements in North America by John Hinton in 1755. Library of Congress, Geographical and Map Division

The shakers and the movers in these colonies knew of the rich lands to their west, and many of them were speculating on large tracts of these western lands which were of course occupied by Native Americans. The British Crown somehow came down on the side of

109 *Inheriting the Trade* by Thomas Norman DeWolf, p 31
110 *New Century History of the United States* by Edward Eggleston, Rev 1916, p 59

the Indians in this matter – perhaps because they also wanted control of these riches. Thomas Jefferson, Patrick Henry, George Mason, George Washington, and most of the other Virginia leaders were the men coordinating the protests against the English western border policy in the years 1774 to 1776, while they speculated extensively in Indian lands across the Appalachians into what would become Kentucky and Ohio.[111] If the Crown had prevailed, these men stood to lose a fortune. We must realize there was more than just freedom on their minds as the Revolution broke out.

There were plenty of stories of Indian atrocities that white men used to justify their deeds. Even as I grew up in the 1950s how often did I hear someone else say "the only good injun is a dead injun"? But consider the Cherokee, a peaceful people that had adapted to our language, higher learning, and even used our form of government by the 1830s. The Cherokee people were marched out of Georgia on the "trail of tears" simply because we wanted their land as a means of great wealth to grow cotton.[112] Our US Government voted to extradite the Cherokee against the will of 15,000 of them that signed a petition to Congress protesting the action. The US Supreme Court ruled that the Cherokee had absolute right to their land – but President Jackson refused to enforce the Court's decision. The Cherokee were forcibly removed from their native land in Georgia and marched 1,000 miles to the west, a most perfect example of ethnic cleansing. Twenty percent of the Cherokee people perished in the process.

We pushed Native Americans from sea to shining sea with less consideration than if we were driving livestock. In the end, we forced them onto reservations, sort of like concentration camps. When the Indians finally stopped pushing back sometime after Custer's Last Stand, it was simply because there were not enough of them left to cause a fuss. Over the course of 250 years we witnessed, presided over, and in many cases directly caused the extermination of one of the great people's of the world, simply because we wanted what they had -- and we had the means to take it.

For all our effort to normalize our relationships with minorities, I cannot see how we have done much to make the same effort with Native Americans. Many still live on reservations, and I fear we think this is okay because they got bingo. Deep in my heart I pray that we did not allow gambling in the 1990s - just as we provided rum in the 1800s simply as a means of "keeping them quiet down on the reservation". Perhaps Native Americans stay on the reservation because they want nothing more to do with being a part of our society. Who could blame them?

111 *The Unknown American Revolution* by Gary B. Nash, p 169-171
112 *Inheriting the Trade* by Thomas Norman DeWolf, p 60

★   ★   ★   ★   ★

Today we have evolved to accept that the male version of most words and activities includes women as well. After a bit of craziness, we no longer have to say "mailmen and mailwomen" and thankfully the use of the more politically correct "mailpeople" has fallen by the way as well. Even as we read or say the older male-dominated form of words, we accept that women are an equal part of whatever it is. However, our founding fathers were quite literal when they said "all men were created equal". We can see by their actions that women were not given a vote and in most cases not guaranteed the freedoms of our government.

Women didn't get the vote until the 14th Amendment in 1920. In the 1950s women still did what their husbands dictated – mostly without question. This was far more the case in 1776. Women had no vote or any say in the town meetings that determined their fate – and their lot was far more tenuous at that time. Did you know that English common law of the time allowed a husband to beat his wife as long as the stick or club did not exceed the thickness of a male thumb?[113] It is amazing today how often we say "well, a good rule of thumb is (whatever)……" without any clue what it originally meant!

The recent HBO series on John Adams of Massachusetts shows him as a primary force behind our Revolution and our second President. The series portrays a loving relationship with his wife Abigail Adams, who managed the farm and family through John's absence for most of a decade. In March of 1776 even before the Declaration was framed, Abigail wrote seriously to John at the Continental Congress in Philadelphia, saying "In the Code of Laws which I suppose it will be necessary for you to make, I desire you would remember the ladies, and be more generous and favorable to them than your ancestors". She further pressed the issue "Do not put such unlimited power into the hand of the husbands. Remember all men would be tyrants if they could. That your sex are naturally tyrannical is a truth so thoroughly established as to admit of no dispute…".[114] John Adams reply only confirms the male attitude toward female subservience by saying "As to your extraordinary code of laws, I cannot but laugh"[115] and he dismissed the topic entirely. One more quick anecdote – John begrudgingly allowed his oldest daughter to be taught Latin, but warned Abigail not to let the neighbors know "for it is scarcely reputable for the young ladies to understand Latin and Greek".[116]

Today we Americans are very quick to point our finger at other people of the world that abuse their women and treat them as second class citizens. We have only recently become civilized in this matter ourselves, and still today I must worry that my daughter will not be paid equitably simply because she is a woman.[117]

---

113 *The Unknown American Revolution* by Gary B. Nash, p 204
114 Ibid p 203
115 Ibid p 204
116 Ibid p 205
117 *Newsweek*, Even Female Law Partners Suffer Wage Disparities by Jesse Ellison, July 9 2010

★　★　★　★　★

So why have I taken an otherwise quaint bit of storytelling and turned to rubbing your nose in stuff that you may feel is best left buried in the barnyard of history? While reading about the Revolution and Noah Pratt, I was amazed to find every topic I just discussed was also being discussed in the 1770s. If we are to be free ourselves – we must understand our past mistakes and learn to avoid them in our own life. Remember, with great power comes great responsibility. At the most basic level, if we are to wield this power of freedom as individuals and as a nation, we cannot have our own freedom at the expense of others loosing theirs. This perfect balance point of freedom cannot be achieved if any one of us forces our views, moral values, or wants on others against their will, as we have done in the examples just discussed. Most importantly, we cannot use democracy to force our views on others - even if we have enough votes. As John Adams said, "a mob is no less a mob because they are with you". In this regard, we have shown that "we the people" working as a democracy can be as much a demagogue as the worst dictator. The fact we all get to vote doesn't prove we are thinking clearly or dealing with others in an even-handed way. At the risk of raising even more hackles, let's talk about a more current example of this.

After all the persecution the Puritans suffered, when they initially arrived here they were somewhat militant that you had to be a Puritan to live in their colony and towns. In fact, portions of Rhode Island – most especially Providence just a stone's throw from Wrentham – were founded by folks forced out of Massachusetts because they didn't conform to the Puritan's strictest religious teachings. You may also recall we discussed the Puritans eventual decision to separate church and state – a smart move considering up till then they were doing exactly what the King of England had done in the first place, using the power of the government to force religious belief. As we founded our country then, we decided to avoid the problem of government forcing a particular religious belief on the people. Separation of church and state means each of us can choose how to worship – or not – without intrusion by the government. That is of course as long as we're not sacrificing virgins, forcing underage women into "marriage", or causing other harm that violates the law.

However, our separation of church and state is a bit one-sided. In the United States religious groups are protected from government interference, but surprisingly there is no real protection against a religious group that would decide to advance their ideology and force their religious beliefs into our civil laws. I've already noted examples in the world where Islamic groups have taken over their government and forced their religious law as the law of the land. I mentioned earlier the example of a woman sentenced by government courts to be stoned to death as prescribed by Islamic law because she was pregnant out of wedlock – even though it was clear the pregnancy was the result of a brutal rape.

Perhaps you think this only happens in other countries half way around the world, but once again here is an example of our own people trying to force their views on others right here in the USA. There are "pro-life" groups in our country that have worked for decades to try and force their religious belief into law, ending a woman's choice to have an abortion under any circumstance. More recently, these groups are working to legally redefine life as beginning at conception – at the very point of having sex. Combined with outlawing abortion, the affect of this would be that a woman using a douche or the "morning after" pill would be charged with murder. Quite literally, if a woman has sex – she must bear the child – period, end of discussion. Believe it or not, this legal definition can be changed by an appointed bureaucrat, and was seriously considered in the waning days of the last Bush administration which was admittedly pro-life.

Now, in all fairness, the pro-life folks could be on the right side of this argument just as the early anti-slavery activists most certainly were. It is also clear that these folks have the right to speak their mind like any other citizen of our fair country and try to convince the rest of us of the righteousness of their beliefs. However, the people of our country are pretty evenly split on the issue of abortion, and I don't think most of us are even aware of a movement to change the legal definition of "life" to the strictest possible religious interpretation. I also cannot help but notice that many of the pro-life events and demonstrations seem to reflect a certain militancy about their opinions and approach to this issue. We have seen large blocks of voters willing to vote in lock-step focused on this issue alone – ignoring all other issues and qualifications. It seems they do not care if we elect the most qualified candidate – only the one that is pro-life. An even more militant side of the pro-life movement is a willingness to bomb clinics and murder in order to further their beliefs. The extreme pro-life view refuses abortion even if the woman was raped or found that her own life is threatened by childbirth. Ultimately, they would strip the right and freedom of a woman to make this most personal decision for herself. How is this so different from radical Islam?

What if the pro-life movement was somehow able to force their beliefs into law? Realizing they may not be able to convince the majority of our citizens to vote to outlaw abortion, the pro-life camp has more recently moved to elect a president who promises to select pro-life appointees to the Supreme Court in order to overturn Roe v Wade. Thus, in the incredibly close 2004 election a couple of normally Democratic states were tilted Republican by pro-life churches making it clear to their congregation that they "must vote their conscience" and turned the election for George W. Bush. If our government cannot interfere with religious activity, how is it religious groups are allowed to meddle in our government and try to force their views on the whole of our population? Apparently the only control on this activity is an administrative rule that a church cannot preach to vote for one candidate over another – thus their demand that the congregation "vote your conscience" (wink, wink). Churches that openly step over this line can only be punished by taking away their non-tax status, nothing more than a slap on the hand.

Once again, we cannot have our own freedom at the expense of others loosing theirs. This perfect balance point of freedom cannot be achieved if any one of us forces our views, moral values, or wants on others against their will. As we become more aware of what is happening in politics today, we will find many examples of this going on around us. Only if the majority of us are informed and willing to assert our views can we prevent such happenings.

★   ★   ★   ★   ★

One of my long time favorite bit of song lyrics plays "still we are free, no one tells the wind which way to blow…" from the Moody Blues album, ironically titled *Question of Balance*.[118] This album, whose title cut was their signature close at concerts, is focused on personal freedom and our relationship with those around us – topics that were so alive following the summer of love as the Vietnam war raged. The final cut talks about us finding compassion and understanding in dealing with others – and therein lies the balance. No matter if we are speaking of balance with your lover, nature, or politics what we are talking about is made of the same stuff. Our freedom is perched on this precipice – this perfect balance point where each of us common men and women must consider other viewpoints with compassion and understanding, or freedom is diminished. Our freedom is the sum of the smallest examples of this for each of us to maintain our "life, liberty, and pursuit of happiness".

My freedom to ride is important to me, even if the majority of the population might take issue with the elements of danger, the lack of a helmet, the noise, the tattoos, or any other aspect of the biker lifestyle they might find offensive. Bikers are an almost perfect cross-section of peace loving, law-abiding citizens, and most of them have a heart as big as all of outdoors. Bikers get involved in helping disadvantaged children, and ride to raise funds for muscular dystrophy, cancer, and diabetes research. Even still, there is an uneasiness surrounding biker issues and we are a small percent of the population – and so we continue to be an easy mark for legislation.

The fact that I choose to ride without a helmet, which is legal in most states, may not be to your liking, but truth is I am not hurting anyone else by exercising this freedom. The fact that you may easily be able to muster enough votes to force helmet use doesn't make it right. Why stop there? Why not make us all wear full body armor, and while we're at it let's dictate the same body armor and helmets for every person riding a bicycle or a horse because they are vulnerable too. Even more insidious is when some appointed politician like the head of the National Transportation Safety Bureau tries to force all states to re-enact helmet laws by withholding federal highway funds – a fight that has been going on for a number of years now. Our government needs to be more focused on the big ticket issues like national security and the safety of our food supply and should not be spending our tax dollars trying to mandate helmet use.

---

118 *Question of Balance*, Album by The Moody Blues, 1970

Many communities are considering specific laws to quiet motorcycles to a purr. Many bikers feel that loud pipes save lives by letting car drivers know they are nearby. The truth is that loud pipes are not actually hurting people. They fall under the category of nuisance, a very subjective thing indeed. After years of sitting in our garden near the lake quietly listening to the birds and wind in the leaves, we now have an ice cream truck prowling the neighborhood streets playing the same 30 second electronic ditty over, and over, and over again ad nauseum. While the kiddies are probably excited about hearing this sound night after night, some others might think it is a nuisance. What about the kids screeching at the neighbor's backyard pool? And what about the neighborhood dogs barking at each other all night long – every night? Let's not just have the police stop otherwise law abiding bikers to check their mufflers – as quid pro quo, let's send the police to every home with a decibel meter to make sure no one is stepping out of line. Sounds sort of like a police state when you think of it beyond the bikers viewpoint, doesn't it? Shouldn't our law enforcement officers have more important things to do with their time?

Beyond bikers, there are thousands of examples of this sort of government meddling in our lives. I suggest that each of you look at some aspect of your freedom that you enjoy, and I suspect if you look close enough you will realize there are threats similar to this. We find ourselves in this situation because we pay too many bureaucrats to sit on their ass and think up ways to justify their job and their annual pay increase, even as the common people of our country experience 9% unemployment, foreclosure of their homes, and staggering health care costs (whew, I don't know where all that came from). If we continue doing this our life, liberty, and pursuit of happiness are continually diminished and ultimately lost. As a society we must be compassionate and understanding of each other – there must be a balance of freedom even for the smallest group of us.

★ ★ ★ ★ ★

Just four years after the end of the Revolution, there was an incident in western Massachusetts that sent a chill through the young Republic and played a key role in creating our US Constitution (that most incredible document, not the ship). Each state had been given a portion of the war debt to be repaid to foreign lenders who were demanding payment in hard currency – gold or silver. The Massachusetts legislature dominated by merchants in Boston, taxed every small farmer a portion also demanding payment in gold or silver. As a result, many debt-ridden farmers, who predictably couldn't pay in gold, lost their farms and homes, and were thrown in debtors' prison. Clearly government was not working – not representing the interests of the common man who had just fought a war to protect their property and freedom – only to lose it to their own government. The result was Shays' Rebellion – farmers and common men armed themselves and marched on the state capitol to demand changes in their government.

Common men with guns were used so effectively to make demands on the British and to win our Revolution. Now, it was most uncomfortable to have these same men with guns demanding change of their new government – never mind how reasonable the change being requested might actually have been.

Shays' Rebellion was a primary force in writing the Constitution that same year, and the Bill of Rights two years later, creating a more stable country as a whole and assuring the basic freedom of individuals could not be taken by our government. It is important to note that even with the fear of Shays' Rebellion burned in their mind, the second amendment in the Bill of Rights assured *"the right of the people to keep and bear arms shall not be infringed"*. This has most recently been re-affirmed by the US Supreme Court as the individual right of our common men and women. Thomas Jefferson, author of the Declaration of Independence and soon to be our third President was not alarmed by Shays' Rebellion and indeed celebrated it writing to a friend "a little rebellion now and then is a good thing. The tree of liberty must be refreshed from time to time with the blood of patriots and tyrants."[119] Thomas Jefferson saw the common man as the ultimate and final 'checks and balances' against a government run amuck.

As I set out to write my book, the word "Revolution" in the title was certainly in reference to our War for Independence. However, as I come to the end – most especially with the thoughts of this chapter in mind - I find myself thinking about Thomas Jefferson. If he were here today, he would be calling for rebellion - a New American Revolution - for every one of us to answer the call and get more involved in determining what our government and our freedom means to us today. In his time Jefferson was not a friend of big government and there were heated discussions with Washington, Adams, and Hamilton about what government should be – just as there are today. Because of these differences our Constitution and Bill of Rights were hammered out through the art of compromise – an art we seem to have lost entirely over the last decades.

If our tree of liberty is to be refreshed, we cannot have a revolution focused only on our own individual wants and needs any more than our founding fathers could have back then. We must look compassionately at all our men and women who were created equal and strive for ways to make government and freedom work for all of us. I hope that today we have come to an understanding that life, liberty, and the pursuit of happiness are not to be enjoyed only by the wealthy and powerful of our society.

Perhaps we could begin a new discourse involving all of us, just as Noah Pratt and Cesar Chelor were involved in their town hall meetings to determine their own destiny. Perhaps we could see a groundswell of renewed interest in this revolution. Perhaps our youth could rise to fill our government with new blood and find a way to break the dysfunction and gridlock that have crippled us for so long. Perhaps patriotism could be back in fashion, and we could see a renewed interest in the stories of our Revolution as an inspiration to the work that must be done. How great it would be if each of us could find a way to celebrate and enjoy our freedom every day we live -- to remind us of how important the work is ahead of us.

---

119 *Give me Liberty! An American History*, Eric Foner 2006, p219

It is mid-October and the color of the trees is long at peak. Today I had the ride of my life winding through my favorite country roads. The welcome sun filtered through thinned tree crowns more than would be the case in summer. The air was fresh and the wind blew leaves off the trees one wave after another falling all around me – I could almost reach out and catch one. Whenever I rode past a small pile on the road the leaves danced in my rearview mirror as the backwash of my bike stirred them into a frenzy. Life is so good as I head towards home to sit in the garden with my wife at the end of a golden afternoon. I am rich beyond measure.

Just like writing my book, instinctively I know the riding season is coming to an end. As I get ready to lay my bike up for storage each year, I always notice my license plate LSTYR which commemorates my 2003 Heritage Springer as the last year Harley-Davidson built this model. It is arguably the most beautiful motorcycle the Motor Company has ever built and I'm lucky to have one. Although the license was purchased to celebrate that last year of production, each year as I get ready to cover the bike for winter, I pray that this was not the last year I will have to enjoy this freedom.

As I researched, and the more I learned about the miracle of the first year of the Revolution surrounding Boston, the more I realized that this bit of history was a big part of Noah's story. Then I came to realize that Noah and his neighbors were a big part of how it happened – just as we could be today. I also realized that their view of freedom was so much more alive than our textbook view of it today. So, I decided to explore the Revolution and Noah Pratt's lifework. I played this against the incredible freedom I enjoy riding my Harley -- offered as a metaphor for your freedom as well, if you will. I realized from the onset this was an unlikely combination of topics, and I pray I've had some success in sharing them with you. If I have not stirred some inner need for you to learn to ride with me on the open road enjoying this beautiful country, at least I hope you begin to understand why bikers are so passionate about our ride, and you will continue to allow us this freedom that is so much a part of our life.

12   Matching the Maker with the Mark

The cherry crown moulding plane that is so central to my story (shown at right) has an N*P makers mark on the toe that has not been documented prior to this book. Tool collectors will appreciate the information I share here, showing that Noah Pratt was in fact the N*P who made this plane. If you are even a bit interested in old planes or enjoy watching the show *History Detectives*, then I invite you to read along. First, a bit of background on planes of this region and period.

Most of the planes found at flea markets today were made in the 1800's by tradesmen who specialized in planemaking for a living. These planes were mostly made of beech wood, were a standard length of 9.5 inches and had narrow rounded chamfers[120] and were lacking in any other artistic detail. These planes were pretty plain, if you'll pardon the pun and the alliteration.

In contrast, the planes we've studied are from the 1700's New England. Many of these makers were trained in the art of building homes or furniture and did beautiful work in addition to making planes. Their planes were longer, made of birch or fruitwood, and often included artistic details unique to the individual planemaker. Pictured here are some New England planes and a common plane from the 1800's at the far right for comparison.

You can see these New England planes featured wide flat chamfers and a hand carved decorative flute or lambs tongue on the front corner at the bottom of the chamfer, most distinctive on Jo Fuller's plane at the center of the group. This detail was originally found on timberframed posts in England.

Figure 44: New England planes from left are from the 1700's include Francis Nicholson, Cesar Chelor, Jo Fuller, Henry Pratt, and an Ohio Tool from the 1800's. Author's collection, photo by Bob Poull

---

120 A chamfer is a means of softening the sharp corner of a piece of wood, see picture above.

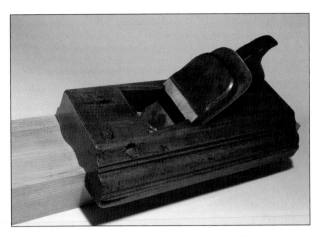

As I began my research, I showed my plane to a number of experts and there was general agreement it is from the 1700's New England area. The wide flat chamfers along the edge of the plane, along with the decorative moulding details and the fact it is made of cherry all support this assumption. However, the entire 1700s is a long time, and we can narrow this down a bit.

Figure 45: (above) Noah Pratt crown moulding plane. (at right) side view showing "mouse-ear tote". Author's collection, photos by Bob Poull

There was a period of time when some of the New England makers added more decorative details to their planes such as the lambs tongue shown on the previous page. These include moulding details added to the side of the plane and occasionally a more decorative handle that collectors affectionately call the "mouse-ear tote" (handle) as seen on my crown moulder here. The time period for this is loosely stated from 1770 to 1800.

During this period many colonial planes were made by what we call "maker / users" meaning the planemaker made it for his own use while doing other woodworking. The N*P mark on this plane fits this description considering it has only initials rather than the whole name that a full time planemaker would have relied on for repeat business. Moreover, the fine details of the plane say the maker was used to doing work of beauty, and the large size of the crown moulding suggests the maker built home interiors or unusually large furniture.

Summarizing to this point, we can tell from the plane itself that it came from New England in the period of 1770-1800 and was likely made by someone who also built homes and/ or furniture.

★ ★ ★ Evidence from American Wooden Planes ★ ★ ★

As mentioned earlier in my book, the essential bible of wooden plane collectors is A Guide to the Makers of *American Wooden Planes*[121] which has no mention of a maker N*P. A thorough reading of the "P" section offers no better clue in this time period in New England than Henry Pratt with a mention of at least one plane made of cherry, and at least one plane marked IN WRENTHAM. Henry is of course the oldest son of Noah Pratt as documented in detail in Chapter 9.

As discussed earlier, the primary area of influence for planemakers in this period was centered in Wrentham, Massachusetts with Francis Nicholson and his freed slave Cesar Chelor. A number of early planemakers lived in a radius centered on Wrentham from the outskirts of Boston down to Providence, RI. Indeed, *American Wooden Planes* confirms that the majority of makers that have a plane noted in cherry, most of the makers adding decorative details to their planes, and all of the planes with a "mouse-ear" tote lived in a 40 mile radius of Wrentham and made planes through the years of 1770-1800. Considering the N*P crown moulder has all three of these, it is reasonable to consider the plane came from this immediate area.

★ ★ ★ Evidence from Noah Pratt and his son Henry ★ ★ ★

We know from historical documents referenced throughout my book that Noah Pratt lived in Wrentham from 1770 to 1792 and worked as a housewright and joiner (furniture maker). It was typical for a craftsman with Noah's skills to also know how to make planes. However, the strongest proof that Noah Pratt made the N*P crown is the life and work of his sons.

Henry and Nathan Pratt were Noah's two oldest sons and they both made planes marked with their name. As discussed in Chapter 9, we know from Henry's work that he built some of the first organs made here in the United States. We can see by his organs that survive that Henry was a consummate craftsman. The first US census in 1790 shows that Henry lived at home through the years he would have apprenticed, and we know Henry moved with Noah and the family to Winchester and continued working in his father's shop. Given these facts, it is certain that Henry and Nathan both learned to make planes along with the trades of housewright and furniture from Noah – a common practice of the time.

Figure 46: Father & son planes. Although Henry's plane at right may have been made decades later, he copied his father's use of cherry and note the wide chamfer which is unusual on a plane made past 1800. Author's collection, photo by Bob Poull

---

121 *American Wooden Planes* by Emil & Martyl Pollak, 4th Edition Revised by Thomas L. Elliott

★ ★ ★ The Chelor connection ★ ★ ★

The most compelling evidence that the N*P crown moulder was made by Noah Pratt in Wrentham is the "mouse-ear" tote (handle) on his plane. (The modern term for this is a bit whimsical in reference to the intersection of the mouse ears on the top of a Mickey Mouse hat.) While doing early research, I bumped into another serious collector at an auction out East carrying a Chelor crown moulder, and we both noted that the handles on the Chelor and N*P planes were essentially identical, as shown below. You may recall we introduced Cesar Chelor, a noted planemaker from Wrentham, Massachusetts, back in Chapter 3.

This handle style is entirely uncommon - only a few makers used it. There is no question that Noah Pratt knew Cesar Chelor. They attended meeting (church) in Wrentham together every week for 14 years before Chelor died in 1784. Moreover, it is likely they visited each other's shop on occasion considering they lived only a couple miles apart as shown back in Figure 11. Craftsmen have forever influenced each other's work, and it is entirely possible Noah Pratt copied the handle from a template on Chelor's bench. We'll never know the extent of influence Cesar Chelor and Noah Pratt had on each other, but a recent article shows that Chelor did add a bit more ornament to a few of his planes in this same time period.[122] Nothing in Chelor's past experience would suggest adding more artistic ornamentation because he only made planes for a living, so he may well have taken the thought from what he saw in Noah Pratt's work.

Figure 47: "mouse-ear" tote (handle) on Noah Pratt plane (at left) and Cesar Chelor plane (above). Pratt plane in the author's collection, photo by Bob Poull. Chelor plane and photo courtesy of the Charles Granick collection.

---

122 *Chelor's Delux Version Planes* by David V. Englund, EAIA Chronicle, March 2006

★ ★ ★ A Call for Additional Information ★ ★ ★

While certainly uncommon, there must be other planes marked N*P and H. PRATT and NATHAN PRATT stuck on collector's shelves around the country. Moreover, I have not been able to find Noah Pratt's home in Wrentham, and as outlined earlier we know his home in Winchester NH was burned to the ground a while ago. Anyone with one of these planes, or who knows of a home that might have been built by Noah Pratt in Wrentham MA 1770-1791 or Winchester NH 1792-1807 could add to the knowledge I've shared here in this book. It is also possible that someday we will find an old organ made by Henry Pratt with a crown moulding large enough to have been done with Noah's plane. I would love to provide a new chapter with additional information on the Pratt family in my book Volume 2 at some point in the future. I would most appreciate corresponding with anyone and I can be reached via the 'Contact' tab on my website and blog at

www.MotorcyclesPlanesandRevolution.com

Thank You

Index